The Battle of West Point

Confederate Triumph at Ellis Bridge

John McBryde

Series Editor Douglas Bostick

The History Press

Published by The History Press
Charleston, SC 29403
www.historypress.net

Cover image: *Gray Wall* by Don Troiani.

First published 2013

Manufactured in the United States

ISBN 978.1.60949.987.7

Library of Congress CIP data applied for.

Notice: The information in this book is true and complete to the best of our knowledge. It is offered without guarantee on the part of the author or The History Press. The author and The History Press disclaim all liability in connection with the use of this book.

Several people in my life have contributed much to the writing and production of this book. Without them, this book would not have come to fruition. I would like to first dedicate this book to my mother, Mrs. Pat McBryde, who pushed me while growing up to work hard and succeed. Her encouragement made me strive to make something out of life. I would also dedicate this book to my grandmother, Mrs. Sally Davis, who told me stories of historical events that made me want to read history; I later developed my own desire to study the history of our past, especially the history of the American Civil War. She told me stories of her grandfather, who fought at Wilson's Creek. Finally, I would like to dedicate this book to Mrs. Esther Pippin, my junior high school librarian, who encouraged me to read all types of books but could never get me away from historical books. She inspired me to read everything I could put my hands on. All three of these women encouraged me through the years to read and to study. They all contributed to my determination to write this history.

Contents

Foreword

The year 1864 was the hardest and most decisive year of the Civil War. Although the majority of the war's bloodiest battles came earlier, 1864 stands out as the worst year of our worst war.

The previous year left the Confederacy reeling from three separate disasters: the defeat at Gettysburg, the surrender at Vicksburg and the loss of Chattanooga. With the strategic initiative now firmly in the grasp of the Federal government, the Confederacy could do little more than prepare for a defensive struggle against odds heavier than those in 1863. The Federal campaigns led to fierce combat, unprecedented in several ways. For one, the fighting in 1864 was relentless and intensive. Once the major field armies met, respites were few and far between. Second, the fighting was extensive—seemingly everywhere in what remained of the Southern Confederacy. By war's end the following spring, only Alabama and Florida had escaped the march of major armies. Third, 1864 marked the first full application of "total war" on Southern civilians. Civilians in north Georgia, Atlanta, the Shenandoah Valley, along William Tecumseh Sherman's route to the sea and throughout wide areas of South Carolina all felt the impact of hard war. Finally, the character of war became more desperate than ever before. In the Union, President Abraham Lincoln faced uncertain reelection. In an increasingly unpopular war, he would need significant and impressive victories. President Jefferson Davis, by contrast, faced no electoral challenge. He faced the defeat of his country. The disasters of 1863, the loss of much of the Confederate "heartland" and the declining source of manpower all combined to put the Confederacy's life on the line.

With large parts of Arkansas, Kentucky, Louisiana, Maryland, Missouri, even Texas and especially Tennessee under Federal occupation, Confederate soldiers from those states found the Federals between them and their homes.

Historians have well recognized and described these realities in a large number of excellent studies of the campaigns of 1864. What has not been generally recognized, however, is that all of it—intensive fighting, extensive fighting and "total war" in increasingly desperate circumstances—began in Mississippi. And the spring campaigning season came early in Mississippi—in February, in fact. General William T. Sherman's Meridian Campaign was the first campaign of the war's worst year.

His campaign was aimed at Meridian, an important railroad junction in southeast Mississippi, and at the Mississippi Black Prairie country in northeast Mississippi. Both were important logistically to the Confederate Army of Tennessee, which would be hard-pressed to defend Atlanta. Sherman planned a two-pronged campaign: he would lead infantry east from Vicksburg to Meridian, while General William S. Smith would lead cavalry south from Memphis, through the Prairie, to rendezvous with Sherman at Meridian. Selma, or even Mobile, loomed as possible further objectives.

The South summoned up its last resources and energy throughout 1864. Again it began in Mississippi, in February. Generals Nathan Bedford Forrest and Stephen D. Lee organized the defense of the Black Prairie. To do it, Forrest would have to recruit his new command—in west Tennessee, from behind Federal lines and in the dead of winter. He came to dominate this campaign, as he dominated my earlier book on the Meridian Campaign (February 27, 1864), *The Battle of Okolona: Defending the Mississippi Prairie* (The History Press, 2009). In this study at the opening of the campaign, leading to the Battle of Ellis Bridge (February 21, 1864), John McBryde introduces the campaign in the Prairie, as well as Forrest at the beginning of his greatest year as a soldier, in the worst year of our worst war.

Brandon Beck
February 26, 2013

Acknowledgements

Several people have contributed much to the formation of this book. I would like to thank the staff of the Chancery Clerk's office and Mr. Robbie Robinson for giving me access to the land deeds of Clay County. I found out a lot about the early settlers of Clay County and the land held by the Ellis family along Sakatonchee Creek. I would like to thank the staff of Bryan Public Library in West Point for contending with me as I spent countless hours in the Local History Room of the library researching the history of the area in 1864. I would like to thank the staff of the Special Collections at Mitchell Memorial Library at Mississippi State University for helping me research letters as well as journals of individuals who resided in West Point when the Federal army invaded the area in 1864. I would also like to thank Brandon Beck for encouraging me to write this story, especially after he published *The Battle of Okolona*. I would also like to thank him for allowing me to use pictures from his book.

To help me understand the battle, I have had the privilege to walk over the area where the fighting actually took place west of West Point. I would like to thank the owner of the land and his son-in-law, Mr. Billy Ross, for making it possible for me to view the land. If there is anyone else who contributed to this book by giving me insight into the battle, I would like to thank you. Most of all, I would like to thank my wife, Janet McBryde, for putting up with me while I spent countless hours researching and writing this book. She has shown a lot of patience with me and given me encouragement along the way.

Introduction

All history teaches that no enemy is so insignificant as to be despised and neglected by any power however formidable.

—Jomini

The Battle of Ellis Bridge, or the Battle of West Point, was the result of a whole series of events that preceded it. Most of these events involved Confederate cavalry General Nathan Bedford Forrest. Up until 1864, Forrest had not yet come into his own as a famous general in the Civil War. Following the Battle of Chickamauga, General Forrest's fate changed. His whole career from the conclusion of Chickamauga to the end of the war made him famous in households all over the Deep South. He became feared by Union generals, especially Sherman, who even commented that he wanted Forrest taken out of the picture. He had a deep respect for Forrest's ability to attack unexpectedly with devastating force.

On the evening following the Battle of Chickamauga, upon the request of General Braxton Bragg, General Nathan Bedford Forrest met with Bragg. Entering Bragg's tent, an exchange of words took place between the two men. Before it was over, Forrest departed Bragg's army with only a handful of men, who eventually became the core of the most dreaded cavalry force in Mississippi, Tennessee and Alabama.

As a result of Bragg transferring Forrest's command to General Joseph Wheeler, Forrest lashed out at Bragg. Forrest would work with other commands; however, he functioned better when his own command was

Confederate General Nathan Bedford Forrest. *Library of Congress.*

Confederate General Braxton Bragg. *Library of Congress.*

independent of everyone else. He especially refused to be placed under Wheeler. These events led to Forrest's transfer to Mississippi.

During the Meridian Campaign, Forrest was everywhere, managing every move of his men and making sure they were in the right place at the right time to counter any movements of the Federal cavalry. He wanted to make sure every detail was attended to so the Federals were not able to get behind him or around him to continue their southerly march to Meridian. This is what made him a great general. He would always outthink his enemies in order to stay ahead of them; they could not outflank, outfight or outwit him. The Federals never knew where he was, but Forrest knew where they were.

Forrest was six feet, one and a half inches tall. He had broad shoulders and a full chest, with symmetrical, muscular limbs. He stood erect in his carriage. His average weight was 185 pounds. He had dark gray eyes, "singularly bright and searching, dark hair, mustache, and beard worn upon the chin, a set of regular white teeth, and clearly cut, sun-embrowned features."[1] He was an impressive figure on horseback. When riding into battle, his whole six-foot frame would stand up in the saddle, making Forrest look like a giant.

On June 14, 1861, Forrest enlisted in the army as a private in Captain Josiah White's Tennessee Mounted Rifle Company. Later, this company became part of the 7th Tennessee Regiment of Cavalry. Forrest had published a notice in the *Memphis Daily Appeal* to secure enlistments for a proposed command that he was trying to raise:

> *Having been authorized by Governor Harris to raise a battalion of mounted rangers for the war, I desire to enlist five hundred able-bodied men mounted and equipped with such arms as they can procure (shotguns and pistols preferable), suitable to the service. Those who cannot entirely equip themselves will be furnished arms by the state. When mustered in, a valuation of the property in horses and arms will be made, and the amount credited to the volunteers. Those wishing to enlist are requested to report themselves at the Gayoso House, where quarters will be assigned until such time as the battalion is raised.*[2]

Forrest raised an army of about 790 men. He outfitted them with weapons and supplies that he procured in Kentucky. Forrest was assigned to Fort Donelson. When General Grant attacked Fort Donelson with a massive army, Forrest escaped the doomed stronghold with nearly 1,500 men as

Grant surrounded the fort. He slipped through Grant's lines, leading these men to safety.

Following Donelson, Forrest participated in the Battle of Shiloh, where he was severely wounded. He pursued General Abel Streight across Alabama. Finally, he ended up at Chickamauga.

CHICKAMAUGA CAMPAIGN

Chickamauga was a creek in northern Georgia south of Chattanooga, Tennessee. A battle was fought there between September 18 and 20, 1863. Repercussions involving Generals Bragg and Forrest set into motion a series of events leading to the subject of this book: Ellis Bridge.

Chickamauga began on Friday, September 18, 1863. In his book *That Devil Forrest*, John Allen Wyeth described the Southern cavalry as having "acquitted itself with credit"[3] in this three-day battle. They were not beaten anywhere on the field. Some attribute the opening shots of the war to Forrest's men, as well as the closing shots of the battle. "On the right [flank] it may be said that Forrest struck the first and the last blow—firing the opening and the final shots in this engagement. He acquitted himself with such distinction as to attract the general attention of the Southern people, and once more to win a special vote of thanks from the Congress of the Confederate States."[4]

When the battle was almost over, Forrest was chasing the retreating enemy toward Chattanooga on September 30 when he received a dispatch from General Bragg, who issued the following order:

> *Missionary Ridge, September 28, 1863*
>
> *Brigadier-General Forrest, near Athens*
>
> *General—The general commanding desires that you will without delay turn over the troops of your command, previously ordered, to Major-General Wheeler*[5]

Forrest lost his temper upon receiving Bragg's dispatch. In response, he dictated a letter to Major Anderson. He admonished Bragg for taking away his troops. In his letter, Forrest charged the commander of the army in plain, straight language with duplicity and lying. He informed Bragg that he would call at his headquarters in a few days to say to him in person just what he had written.[6]

Dr. Cowen, Forrest's chief surgeon, was the only one to accompany him to Bragg's headquarters on Missionary Ridge. Upon entering Bragg's tent, General Bragg offered his hand to Forrest, but Forrest

> [r]*efused to take the proffered hand, and standing stiff and erect before Bragg, Forrest said "I am not here to pass civilities or compliments with you, but on other business. You commenced your cowardly and contemptible persecution of me soon after the battle of Shiloh, and you have kept it up ever since. You did it because I reported to Richmond facts, while you reported damned lies. You robbed me of my command in Kentucky, and gave it to one of your favorites—men that I armed and equipped from the enemies of our country. In a spirit of revenge and spite, because I would not fawn upon you as others did, you drove me into west Tennessee in the winter of 1862, with a second brigade I had organized, with improper arms and without sufficient ammunition, although I had made repeated applications for the same. You did it to ruin me and my career. When in spite of all this I returned with my command, well equipped by captures, you began again your work of spite and persecution, and have kept it up; and now this second brigade, organized and equipped without thanks to you or the government, a brigade which has won a reputation for successful fighting second to none in the army, taking advantage of your position as the commanding general in order to further humiliate me, you have taken these brave men from men. I have stood our meanness as long as I intend to. You have played the part of a damned scoundrel, and are a coward, and if you were any part of a man I would slap our jaws and force you to resent it. You may as well not issue any more orders to me, for I will not obey them, and I will hold you personally responsible for any further indignities you endeavor to inflict upon me. You have threatened to arrest me for not obeying your orders promptly. I dare you to do it, and I say to you that if you every again try to interfere with me or cross my path it will be at the peril of your life.*[7]

Concluding his outburst, Forrest stormed out of Bragg's tent. Dr. Cowan said to Forrest, "Well, you are in for it now!" Forrest's reply to Cowan was, "He'll never say a word about it; he'll be the last man to mention it; and, mark my word, he'll take no action in the matter. I will ask to be relieved and transferred to a different field, and he will not oppose it."[8]

FORREST'S TRANSFER OF OPERATIONS

Forrest, while stationed at Kingston, Tennessee, sent a proposal to President Davis on August 9, 1863, describing a plan for him to be transferred to north Mississippi and west Tennessee, where he would begin operations against Union troops in the area:

> *General—Prompted by the repeated solicitations of numerous friends and acquaintances resident in West Tennessee and Northern Mississippi, also by desire to serve my country to the best of my ability, and wherever those services can be rendered most available and effective, I respectfully lay before you a proposition which, if approved, will seriously, if not entirely, obstruct the navigation of the Mississippi river, and in sixty days procure a large force now inside the enemy's lines, which without this, or a similar move, cannot be obtained.*[9]
>
> *The proposition is this: Give me the command of the forces from Vicksburg to Cairo, or, in other words, all the forces I may collect together and organize between those points—say in Northern Mississippi, West Tennessee, and those that may join me from Arkansas, Mississippi and southern Kentucky. I desire to take with me only about four hundred men from my present command—viz, my escort, sixty: McDonald's battalion, one hundred and fifty; the Second Kentucky Cavalry, Two hundred and fifty—selected entirely on account of their knowledge of the country in which I propose to operate. In all, say, men and outfit, four hundred men, with long-range guns (Enfield), four three-inch Dahlgren or Parrott guns, with eight number-one horses to each gun and caisson, two wagons of the battery, one pack mule to every ten men, and two hundred rounds of ammunition for small arms and artillery.*[10]

Forrest's proposal gives a general idea of what he intended to do once in western Tennessee and northern Mississippi. He wanted to amass a rather large force of mounted horsemen to take the fight to Federal troops, as well as protect the area from invasion. Forrest felt he could do this and do it well because of his previous knowledge of the area having been a citizen from this part of the South.

While decisions were being made in regard to Forrest's change in field of operations, Federal General Grant had given up on invading Mississippi by land. Grant decided to use the Mississippi River as an alternative route for taking Mississippi. President Davis, knowing about Grant's plan for an invasion of Mississippi, felt Forrest could complicate Grant's plans.

On October 29, Forrest received a message from Davis, who directed him to proceed at once to his new assignment. Along with Forrest, Major McDonald's battalion (139 men), Forrest's escort company (65 men) along with his field and staff (81 men) and Captain's J.W. Norton's battery (61 men) accompanied him to Mississippi.

Once Forrest arrived at his new assignment, General Joe E. Johnston ordered him to proceed to raise new troops for the Confederacy. Colonel Richardson, who was already in Okolona, had been ordered to report to Forrest. He was to place his command under Forrest. So, when Forrest arrived in Okolona, Mississippi, he was greeted by Colonel R.V. Richardson and 250 effectives. Forrest wrote to General Johnston about Richardson's command. From his letter, we can surmise that Forrest was disappointed with Richardson's command. Forrest expected to see more men ready to fight when he reached Okolona.

While in Okolona, a dispatch arrived from General S.D. Lee. In his dispatch, Lee wrote, "I am confident that 5,000 men can be raised in West Tennessee. I take this occasion to state, general, that whether you are under my command or not, we shall not disagree, and you shall have all the assistance and support I can render you. I would feel proud either in commanding or co-operating with so gallant an officer as yourself and one who has such an established reputation in the cavalry service."[11] Finally, Forrest had found a friendly commander who would give him the latitude to pursue, attack and defeat the enemy.

General Stephen Dill Lee, painted by John Slato, from the original (1877) by Nicolla Marschall. Photo by Elisa Shizak. *Stephen Dill Lee Home and Museum, Columbus, Mississippi, and Brandon Beck.*

Richardson had a small detachment of troops due to the fact that many of his men had returned home to Tennessee and Mississippi to get warm clothes for winter. Richardson was supposed to have about 800 men but only had 250 when Forrest arrived. He also had 271 guns, 151 pistols and 247 horses available for service.[12]

Another regiment arrived in Okolona with only 150 men—one quarter of them were not armed. Now the total number of troops had reached 700 men. In order for Forrest to break through the Federal lines occupying the Memphis and Charleston Railroad above the Mississippi-Tennessee border, he had to slip through undetected. After crossing the railroad, Forrest rode with his men to Jackson, Tennessee, where he made his temporary headquarters. From there, he began the job of recruiting new troops to add to his present numbers. Forrest first tried to get volunteers. He had made up his mind that if this failed he would resort to conscription.

PRELIMINARY FEDERAL PLANS

What were the Federals doing while Forrest was in Okolona? Federal General Stephen Hurlbut had received word that Forrest was taking charge of Confederate operations in west Tennessee and northern Mississippi. Hurlbut was commander of the Federal district in the Memphis area. Upon hearing of Forrest's presence in the area, he set about pulling together a large force to bottle up Forrest so he could not escape from Tennessee. He also wanted to destroy Forrest's cavalry so he would not have to worry about it moving around his district causing havoc.

Nothing got by Forrest unnoticed. He, too, found out Hurlbut's plans. Hurlbut had Federal troops scattered all along the Memphis and Charleston Railroad in force. Forrest also learned that a strong Federal force was about to move down from Columbus, Kentucky; another from the direction of Fort Pillow; and another from Corinth. They were all going to converge on the area where Forrest was recruiting and attempt to wipe out his Confederate force.[13]

A progression of events followed leading up to January 1864, when the Meridian Campaign was planned and eventually put into motion. Both armies were placed in their positions, according to the *Official Records* of the war, where their paths would cross as they moved south. They would first meet on the field of battle on February 21, 1864, three miles west of West Point.

We leave Forrest in Como, Mississippi, in December 1863. The Federals are in Tennessee at the end of December and the first of January, preparing to move south. Forrest had sent out scouts to watch the movements of Federal troops. Preparations began in January for the Meridian Campaign, and Confederates began shifting troops to counter any and all movements by the Federals.

The preparations of both armies will be addressed, along with the battle in West Point that ultimately changed the course of the Meridian Campaign and perhaps even prolonged the war in the west for one more year.

Part I

Preparations for a Raid

The best strategy is always to be very strong first in general, and then at the decisive point...There is no higher and simple law of strategy than that of keeping one's forces concentrated.

–*Sun Tzu*

Early in the war, General Winfield Scott, commander of all Union forces, devised a plan to choke the South into submission. His plan became known as the Anaconda Plan because it resembled a South American snake, stretching from the southern ports in the Atlantic and wrapping around Florida and into the Gulf of Mexico. The anaconda then wrapped itself around Mississippi up the Mississippi River. By January 1864, this plan had been accomplished. No supplies were entering the South from overseas ports except by blockade runners. Both the Confederate army and the citizens of the South suffered from the Union blockade.

Federal Division of the South

By January 1864, General Grant desired to further subdivide the South in the Western Theater by sending William T. Sherman on a mission to scorch a swath of land across the southern half of Mississippi and maybe even Alabama. The plans included Sherman occupying Selma and Mobile,

Federal General Ulysses S. Grant. *Library of Congress.*

Federal General William T. Sherman. *Library of Congress.*

Federal General Stephen Hurlbut. *Library of Congress.*

Alabama. The east bank of the Mississippi needed to be cleared of Confederate snipers shooting at Union gunboats and supply boats moving up and down the Mississippi River. Basically, Grant wanted to clear Mississippi of all Confederate opposition. He wanted to take or destroy all Confederate stores supplying the Confederate army. The task fell to Sherman, who at the time was in Knoxville after the Battle of Chattanooga. Sherman was in command of the Department of the Tennessee, "which embraced substantially the territory on the east bank of the Mississippi River, from Natchez up to the Ohio River, and thence along the Tennessee River as high as Decatur and Bellefonte, Alabama."[14] General McPherson was at Vicksburg, and General Hurlbut was at Memphis. They both provided Sherman regular reports concerning Confederates in each of their areas. In his memoirs, Sherman said that there was "a considerable force of infantry and cavalry in the State of Mississippi, threatening the river, whose navigation had become to us so delicate and important matter."[15]

Sherman went to Nashville to meet with General Grant and plead his case. Grant consented to Sherman's plans so that Sherman might "go back to Mississippi, to the limits of his own department and where most of his army still remained, for the purpose of clearing out what Confederate might still be left on the east bank of the Mississippi River to impede its navigation by boats."[16] Sherman and Grant were described as the "Damon and Pythias" of the Union hosts in J.A. Wyeth's *That Devil Forrest*.

Sherman had gone up north to spend Christmas with his wife and then returned by river on the *Juliet* to Memphis, where he arrived on January 10. Once in Memphis, he explained the purpose of his campaign to General Hurlbut. He told him he wanted to march out of Vicksburg to Meridian

Federal General William Sooy Smith. *From Francis Trevelynn Miller's* The Photographic History of the Civil War in Ten Volumes, *vol. 10, courtesy of Brandon Beck.*

to tear up the Mobile and Ohio Railroad and the railroad between Selma and Vicksburg. While in Memphis, Sherman met with Brigadier General W. Sooy Smith, who had a force of 2,500 cavalry. Smith was in Memphis to "punish the rebel General Forrest," who had been most active in harassing "the garrisons in West Tennessee and Mississippi."[17]

On January 27, Sherman embarked for Vicksburg by boat. On February 1, he arrived in Vicksburg, where he met a spy who had been sent out to Meridian two weeks before. He reported to Sherman that General Polk was in chief command, with his headquarters at Meridian; he had two divisions of infantry, one belonging to General Loring and posted at Canton, Mississippi, and the other belonging to General Samuel French, at Brandon.

Confederate General Leonidas Polk. *Library of Congress.*

There were two divisions of cavalry. Armstrong's was composed of three brigades, commanded by Ross, Stark and Wirt Adams. They were scattered from Yazoo City to Jackson and south. The other division belonged to Forrest, who was in Como, Mississippi.

Plans for this expedition called for Sherman to travel from Vicksburg to Meridian and for Sooy Smith to travel from Collierville to Meridian. Both commanders' approach to this expedition was to be one of total war against the populace. Sherman's plans were to wage war on the hostile civilians he encountered along the way. John Marszalek, in *Sherman: A Soldier's Passion for Order*, said that Sherman "sought historical precedents for the treatment of…civilians."[18] This type of war was similar to earlier conflicts in history. Marszalek wrote that the civilians were responsible for their own suffering. He explained, "They had brought on the war, and he refused to be blamed for the legitimate suffering they experienced because of it."[19] When there was revolution in Ireland, British monarchs William and Mary sent armies to put down the revolt; as a result, war was waged against the civilians, and they were driven off their lands and replaced with other settlers.

Sherman believed that if the English could wage war against their people, so he could do against Southerners. Sherman believed that "when the provisions, forage, mules, wagons, are used by our enemy it is clearly our duty and right to take them, because otherwise they might be used against us."[20] As far as women and children in his or Sooy Smith's path, he believed that "so long as non-combatants remain in their houses and keep to their accustomed business their opinions and prejudices can in no wise influence the war, and therefore should not be noticed; but if any one comes out into the public streets and creates disorder he or she should be punished, restrained or banished."[21]

FEDERAL CAVALRY OPERATIONS

Provision for seven thousand cavalry commanded by William Sooy Smith had been made by General Grant; they would leave from Collierville, Tennessee, and travel south through Mississippi to Meridian, where they would join with Sherman in Meridian. Smith was to begin his march on February 1, 1864. At the time these movements were taking place, Forrest had close to four thousand cavalry "composed of thoroughly well-disciplined men, who under so able a leader were very effective."[22] Even though Forrest's men may not have been as experienced as the Federals under Smith, they were excellent at winning decisive victories. Their ability to do this rested totally in Forrest as an effective officer. Once he tasted battle, he did not give in until the battle had been won.

Before Sherman's campaign was set in motion, he issued Special Field Orders No. 11 to his army:

> *The expedition is one of celerity, and all things must tend to that. Corp commanders and staff officers will see that our movements are not encumbered by wheeled vehicles improperly loaded. Not a tent, from the commander-in-chief down, will be carried. The sick will be left behind, and the surgeons can find houses and sheds for all hospital purposes. All cavalry in this department is placed under the orders and command of Brigadier-General W.S. Smith who will receive special instructions.*[23]

This order was followed by a dispatch from Sherman to Brigadier General Smith on January 27, 1864:

> *Dear General: by an order issued this day I have placed all the cavalry of this department subject to your command. I estimate you can make a force of full seven thousand men, which I believe to be superior and better in all respects than the combined cavalry which the enemy has in all the state of Mississippi. I will in person start for Vicksburg today, and with four divisions of infantry, artillery and cavalry move out for Jackson, Brandon, and Meridian, aiming to reach the latter place by February 10th...I want you with our cavalry to move out from Collierville on Pontotoc and Okolona; thence sweeping down near the Mobile & Ohio Railroad, disable that road as much as possible, consume or destroy the resources of the enemy along that road, break up the connection with Columbus, Mississippi, and finally reach me at or near Meridian as near the date I have mentioned as possible.*[24]

There is no doubt that Sherman and Smith knew all about Forrest. They both feared an encounter with him. Forrest's fame went ahead of him wherever he served. Smith and Sherman were not any different. Sherman issued orders to Smith concerning a possible encounter with Forrest:

> *Do not let the enemy draw you into minor affairs, but look solely to the greater objects to destroy his communication from Okolona to Meridian, and*

> *thence eastward to Selma. From Okolona south you will find abundance of forage collected along the railroad, and the farmers have corn standing in the fields. Take liberally of all these, as well as horses, mules, cattle, etc. As a rule, respect dwellings and families as something too sacred to be disturbed by soldiers, but mills, barns, sheds, stables, and such like things use for the benefit or convenience of your command. If convenient, send into Columbus, Mississippi, and destroy all machinery there and the bridge across the Tombigbee, which enables the enemy to draw the resources of the east side of the valley, but this is not of sufficient importance to delay your movement.*[25]

Once all the cavalrymen around Memphis were gathered to participate in the Meridian Campaign under General Sooy Smith, they were delayed while waiting on Colonel George Waring, who had to travel from Columbus, Kentucky, to Collierville. He had to cross swollen rivers and creeks in west Tennessee. Cold weather had caused ice to form on the creeks and roads. That ice was not strong enough to bear the weight of horse or man, but it was thick enough to interfere with swimming or crossing in small ferryboats. Once the weather began to clear up, the creeks and crossings became extremely muddy, making them difficult to ford. The Obion and Hatchie bottoms presented transportation problems due to mud.

Federal Colonel George Waring. *Library of Congress.*

On the evening of February 8, Waring finally arrived in Collierville, but Smith's entire force could not move out until February 11. Waring had to have time before his horses were ready to move. When they arrived on February 8, they were jaded and unable to go any farther. New horseshoes had to be fitted on the horses before they were ready to depart Collierville. Smith "marched out of Collierville at the head of seven thousand picked cavalry, armed with Colt repeating rifles, modern carbines, and army revolvers—in all probability the most formidable cavalry command which had ever been organized in the Western armies. There went with it twenty pieces of artillery."[26]

FORREST'S NEW COMMAND

When Forrest arrived in Tennessee, he began recruiting new troopers. Forrest was met in Jackson, Tennessee, by Colonel Tyree Bell, who was sent there to round up deserters and absentees of Bragg. Knowing Bell was in west Tennessee, Forrest sent a message by courier to Bell to meet him in Jackson. Besides the absentees rounded up by Bell, Colonel Richardson also rounded up several hundred men. By the evening of December 23, Colonel Bell had acquired about 1,600 to 1,700 officers and men. Richardson had added about 1,000 men to his command. Lieutenant Colonel D.M. Wisdom reported to General Forrest with 150 men of Colonel Jeffrey Forrest's old brigade. (The two Forrests were brothers.)

When time came for Nathan Bedford Forrest to break out of west Tennessee back into Mississippi, he used cunning, deception and strategy to force his way back into Mississippi. He had the Tennessee behind him and on his left. The Mississippi was on his right, and in front of him were the Forked Deer, Hatchie and Wolf Rivers. Besides these natural geographical barriers around Forrest, he had to contend with General Stephen Hurlbut in Memphis, who had twenty thousand troops watching the crossings of all the rivers and creeks. Forrest "had Federal troops moving from Union City, Fort Pillow and Paducah, Kentucky, on his flank and rear."[27]

Confederate General James Chalmers. *Library of Congress.*

The "Wizard of the Saddle" had three thousand unarmed men and a heavy train of supplies he had to transfer into Mississippi. Brigadier General James R. Chalmers in the *Southern Historical Society Papers* wrote that "escape would have seems impossible to a less daring and less wary man. But one of the greatest secrets of Forrest's success was his perfect system of scouts."[28] Forrest knew "where his enemy was, what he had, what he was doing and very often for days in advance what he was about to do."[29] The bridge over Wolf River was captured by Forrest's men near Lafayette Station on the Memphis and Charleston Railroad. He held the enemy at bay in Collierville while he passed into Mississippi with 3,500 men, forty wagons loaded with subsistence, two hundred beef cattle and three hundred hogs.[30]

While Forrest was attempting to deceive the Federals while moving his train of men and animals south, Federal troops under A.J. Smith were sent south from Columbus, Kentucky, and William Sooy Smith was to gather a force from middle Tennessee, Kentucky and northern Alabama and then cross the Tennessee River in pursuit of Forrest from the east. Federal Brigadier General Joseph A. Mower was commanded to advance from Corinth, Brigadier General Benjamin Grierson was to advance from the southwest at La Grange and Brigadier General George Crook was to move to Tennessee from Huntsville, Alabama. Hurlbut was of the opinion that he was going to "cure Forrest ambition to command west Tennessee."[31]

Despite all efforts by the Federal army to trap and capture Forrest, he was able to avoid major conflicts between his new recruits and Federal forces. His men fought only minor skirmishes with the Federals. Most of Forrest's men who fought in these were seasoned troops who had seen battle before.

Once Forrest had begun moving his forces, a menagerie of animals and wagon trains south, he sent word to Chalmers, who commanded the cavalry in north Mississippi, to make a demonstration against the Memphis and Charleston Railroad as a decoy to draw the attention of the Federal troops from the railroad so that Forrest, with his vast party, could cross the tracks into north Mississippi unnoticed.

When the breakout into north Mississippi occurred, Forrest headed everyone south toward Holly Springs on December 27, 1863. Forrest left the Federals in Tennessee chasing shadows. Anyone who moved was pursued by the Federals thinking they were Forrest's men.

Brigadier General Chalmers, in a speech to the Southern Historical Society in October 1879, quoted a piece written by a correspondent with the *Cincinnati Commercial* in Memphis on January 12, 1864, about Forrest slipping out of Tennessee: "Forrest with less than four thousand men, has moved right through the Sixteenth Army Corps, has passed within nine miles of Memphis, carried off one hundred wagons, two hundred beef cattle, three thousand conscripts and innumerable stores, torn up railroad track, cut telegraph wire, burned and sacked trains, over pickets with a singled derringer pistol, and all, too, in the face of ten thousand men."[32]

After arriving in Mississippi, Forrest had brought with him from west Tennessee about 3,500 recruits. He moved his camp to Como, Mississippi, where he began fashioning his command into a cohesive fighting force. While in Como, Forrest received a dispatch from Polk's headquarters calling on him to proceed immediately to Canton to meet with Polk and General S.D. Lee. The dispatch was sent to General Forrest on January 25:

> *General Forrest*
> *Como:*
>
> *I desire you, if all is quiet on the Mobile and Ohio Railroad, to relieve General Ferguson and order him with his brigade to report to General Lee. He may report by telegraph and send his guns and baggage by railroad. You will retain with you the regiment of Colonel Barteau. If you find the fortification you speak of evacuated you may destroy them with Gholson and Barteau, and any others you may add to them. Send Ferguson at once. I wish you to visit General Lee and myself at Canton on Thursday.*
>
> *L Polk*
> *Lieutenant-General*[33]

While meeting with Lee and Polk, Forrest learned that a new department had been created. All cavalry commands in west Tennessee and northern Mississippi as far south as a line drawn across the state just to the north of Columbus, Grenada and Cleveland encompassed Forrest's new command. His new command included "the southern boundaries of the counties of Monroe, Calhoun, Chickasaw, Yalobusha, Tallahatchie and a part of Sunflower and Bolivar lying north of a line drawn from the southwest corner of Tallahatchie County to the town of Prentiss, on the Mississippi River, to be known and designated as 'Forrest's Cavalry Department.'"[34]

Included in General Forrest's dispatch to all cavalry within his new district was this directive:

> *All cavalry commanders north of this line will at once report to these headquarters the strength and condition of their commands. The strength of the enemy in our front, and their merciless ravages on this portion of the country during the past two years, should furnish a sufficient appeal to men to rally at once for the defense of their homes. I come to you with a full supply of arm, ammunition, and accoutrements, and there are men enough in the department, if properly organized, to drive the enemy from our soil. Let us then be prompt in our organizations and ready for the spring campaign.*[35]

When Forrest returned to Como, he busied himself with organizing his command by assigning his commanders to four brigades. These four brigades included Brigadier General R.V. Richardson with 1,500 men in five regiments and two separate battalions of west Tennessee troops; Colonel Tyree Bell with 2,000 men in five regiments of Tennessee troops, including Barteau's 2nd Tennessee Cavalry; Colonel Robert McCulloch with 1,200 men in the 2nd Missouri, Falkner's Kentucky Regiment, a battalion of Mississippi cavalry, a Texas battalion, two Tennessee battalions and a fragment of the 2nd Arkansas; and Colonel Jeffrey Forrest with 1,000 men in the 7th Tennessee, three regiments and a battalion of Mississippi troops.[36]

In General Orders No. 2, issued by General Forrest, he assigned the following officers as members of his staff on January 24, 1864, while in Como:

- Major J.P. Strange, assistant adjutant-general
- Captain C.W. Anderson, aide-de-camp
- Lieutenant W.M. Forrest, aide-de-camp
- Dr. J.B. Cowan, chief surgeon
- Major C.S. Severson, chief quartermaster
- Major G.V. Rambaut, chief of subsistence
- Lieutenant T.S. Tate Jr., assistant inspector-general
- Captain George Dashiell, chief paymaster
- Captain J.B. Russell, chief of ordnance[37]

Forrest had problems with the troops he recruited in Tennessee. Many of the regiments he recruited were skeleton organizations, not up to regulation strength. All of these groups had to be molded into "more compact and efficient forms."[38] There were many officers who joined Forrest's recruits without commands. Some of these joined under the assumption that they would receive some type of command position but were disappointed when they found out that they were not going to get a command of a regiment or better. These men were highly discouraged when they did not receive what they thought they deserved. Unfortunately, "this bred a state of discontent and disorganization among the men."[39] Many of the men actually returned to their homes. Forrest sent detachments of his veteran troops out to gather these deserters and bring them back. When they were returned, Forrest placed each of the men into a regiment under a commander. Once the organization of his command had been accomplished, he removed his headquarters to Oxford, Mississippi, which according to Jordan and Pryor was "a more central and favorable point, in view of a possible necessity for cooperation with other Confederate forces against a rumored movement from Vicksburg, northward."[40] The rest of Forrest's command was withdrawn to the south bank of the Tallahatchie and concentrated at Panola under the command of Brigadier General Chalmers.

Problems still existed with some of the men. Some of them wanted to go home to get more clothing for the winter weather. They had been brought south from their homes so fast they did not have time to put together the clothing they needed. Nineteen men went absent without leave from the camp to slip back north to their homes. They were promptly pursued, captured and brought back to camp in disgrace. Their commander gave the order for these men to be shot.

Coffins were made and their graves were dug. Each of the men was told to make peace with his maker. In the meantime, citizens of Oxford heard about the proposed execution. They became indignant about the idea. Many even begged General Forrest to countermand the order. Even some of General Forrest's officers "felt it their duty to inform the General of their serious apprehension of a mutinous resistance on the part of the soldiery to the attempt to execute so many of their comrades."[41]

The condemned prisoners were marched out before the troops, blindfolded and seated on their coffins, and the firing squad was drawn up in front of them waiting for the order to fire. At the moment the order to fire was to be given, Forrest gave all nineteen a reprieve. He remanded them all to prison through one of his staff officers. Forrest did not have any choice but to put these nineteen men through this early on. He had to prove that he was in command and that he expected loyalty and allegiance to him. He could not allow this type of behavior to continue. He had to have a cohesive command that would follow his orders.

After organizing his command, Forrest began issuing orders to his four commanders that would strategically place them in positions to watch for the advance of Federals into north Mississippi. He would not allow his whole army to remain in Como to be trapped nor would he sit idly by while Federal cavalry marched unopposed through Mississippi. Forrest believed wholeheartedly in taking the fight to the enemy first.

Parallel Marches

Owing to the fact that Forrest was not one to sit still and wait on the enemy to attack him first, he proved himself to be as cunning as a fox. He knew Smith's cavalry was preparing to move long before it actually did due to the reports furnished to him by his cadre of scouts. In preparation for Smith's herculean plan, on February 9, General Forrest, then at Oxford, telegraphed Brigadier General Chalmers, who at that time was in Panola. Chalmers was ordered to skirmish with the two Federal infantry columns that had moved out on the eighth toward Panola and Wyatt. Forrest explained to Chalmers the Federal infantry movement was only a feint but Forrest wanted Chalmers to be ready to "intercept the cavalry, which he predicted would strike for Columbus and the Prairie country of east Mississippi, where we had government works and a large quantity of corn."[42]

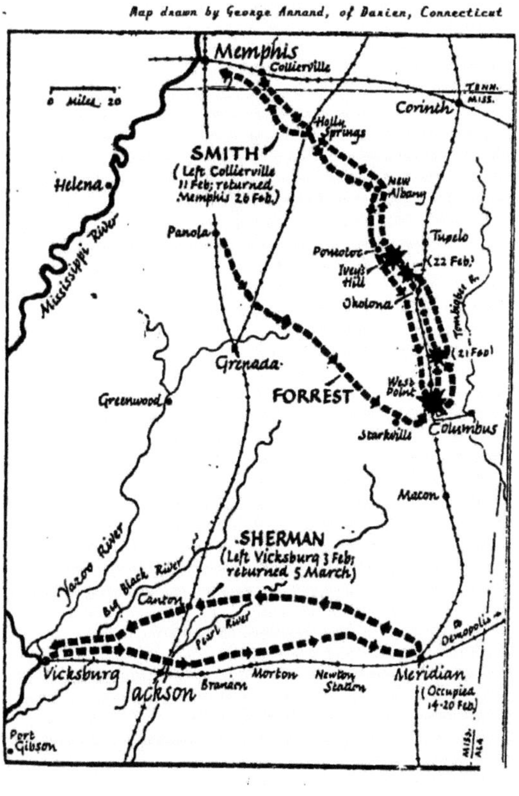

Map outlining the route of Sooy Smith's expedition to West Point. *George Annand.*

Since some of these men were from other units, they had deserted or were without officers who were without commands. Forrest did not have enough command positions to place them, so he demoted them and placed them in units as regular soldiers. Some of these men did not like this, so they left his army.

The second detail Forrest took care of was the amalgamation of troops. He combined Jeffrey Forrest's and Robert McCulloch's brigades to form a division and then placed them under Brigadier General Chalmers's command.

Confederate General Samuel Gholson. *From Francis Trevelynn Miller's* The Photographic History of the Civil War in Ten Volumes, *vol. 10, courtesy of Brandon Beck.*

McCulloch and Richardson were ordered by Forrest to use their brigades to cover an area from Panola to Abbeville. They had to watch the crossings of the Tallahatchie River. Colonel Jeffrey Forrest was ordered to position his brigade at Grenada to watch the forces at Yazoo City. Richardson went to Toby-Tubby, and McQuirk stationed his men at Abbeville. Bell was moved to Belmont.

There is one more Confederate command that played a role in the defense of north Mississippi in February 1864. The 1st Mississippi Partisan Rangers, commanded by General Samuel J. Gholson, took an active role in slowing down Smith's army twice from February 20 to February 22, 1864. Gholson was ordered to lead his force to a strategic position where he could check the forward progress of Sooy Smith's seven thousand Federal cavalrymen. He was ordered to move his command "out to Red land, in the direction of Houston, or even to the right of that," where he "can get forage and be in striking distance"[43] in case Forrest had to fall back.

From Oxford on February 10, General Forrest sent a dispatch to General Polk detailing the then current movements of the enemy:

> *Fifteen hundred infantry and 300 cavalry come out as far as Senatobia. Colonel McCulloch met and drove them back to Hickahale. I think this is*

> *only a feint. Their real move is to go from Collierville to Pontotoc and strike the Prairies and Mobile and Ohio Railroad.* [I] *Am preparing to meet that move as best I can. They have about 10,000 cavalry, and mounted infantry. Smith's Dutch brigade from Columbus passed Somerville on the 7th, going tin direction of Memphis; mounted recently in West Tennessee.*[44]

Preparations already made by Forrest became even more necessary as Forrest determined that the movements of Federal cavalry in and around Memphis were part of a cooperative effort with Sherman, whose objective was Meridian. The Federal forces General Forrest faced in north Mississippi were only a feint to keep his attention diverted from Sooy Smith's main force. The Federal diversion did not fool Forrest because of his scouts, who kept him informed of all Federal troop movements.

As the evening of February 11 arrived, the chief of scouts for Forrest's command, Captain Thomas Henderson, reported that a large column of cavalry from Memphis was heading toward Holly Springs by both the Germantown and Byhalia roads. Brigadier General Chalmers was "instantly instructed to concentrate his entire force at Oxford as soon as possible."[45]

Several skirmishes occurred around Wyatt and Abbeville between Confederate and Federal forces. The Federals were attempting to cross the Tippah River but were denied passage. Faulkner's Kentuckians stopped the Federals from crossing during the night of February 18. While this was taking place, the main force moved around the north side of the Tippah and crossed the countryside toward Pontotoc unopposed. Forrest sent word to General Polk on February 14 from Grenada:

> *Their forces are moving to my right, crossing Tippah today 10 miles above its mouth on the road to New Albany. I am of opinion the larger portion of their forces will move via Pontotoc to Houston or Okolona and thence southward. Their forces are variously estimated at twenty-seven to thirty-one regiments cavalry and one brigade of infantry, thirteen pieces of artillery. From the best information I can get from scouts and other sources, I think they have 10,000 to 12,000 cavalry. Colonel Forrest's and General Chalmers' brigades move this evening to Houston. I have ordered all the balance of my forces to concentrate here and will follow to West Point with all my forces tomorrow. Watch your right wing closely, and have General Lee's forces in position to cooperate with me. In the event the enemy proves too strong for me I shall fall back in the enemy's front toward Meridian, in case I am forced to fall back at all.*[46]

Forrest's suspicions of the Federals' route south were confirmed when they headed toward Pontotoc. He knew then, for sure, that the Federals were heading south to the rich prairie region and to Okolona. He ordered Chalmers to move at once to keep on Smith's right flank. Following Smith on this flank, Chalmers headed toward Houston, which was forty-five miles southeast of Oxford. Chalmers arrived in Houston on February 14, late in the evening. General Forrest had sent a report to General Polk on February 15 describing his movements up to February 15 in Grenada:

> *My scouts report the enemy, 10,000 strong, crossing at New Albany on 13th and 14th with thirty pieces of artillery. I fear they are ahead of me. General Chalmers brigade is moving to Houston from Oxford. Colonel Forrest's brigade left here yesterday, and I think will reach West Point by 2 am tomorrow. I move from here with Bell's and Richardson's brigades at 4 o'clock in the morning, and will endeavor to fall in about Starkville.*[47]

General Forrest, as this dispatch reported, left for Grenada with Bell's Brigade, his escort and the artillery along with Richardson's brigade. Colonel Jeffrey Forrest was already in Grenada but was ordered to move toward the east to West Point on the Mobile and Ohio Railroad, the area being threatened by a possible invasion by General Smith and his seven thousand cavalry. Once Colonel Forrest arrived in West Point, he was to set up a line of couriers between West Point and Houston to establish communication between Colonel Forrest and Chalmers in Houston. General Forrest gave this order to Chalmers because he had determined that the purpose of the enemy was to move in the direction of Okolona and Meridian. The general wanted Chalmers to "keep his force in hand to grapple with such a movement."[48]

Okolona was a dividing line between the hill country and the flat country. Okolona was an Indian name that meant "Queen of the Prairie."[49] If one toured this country, especially along the Mobile and Ohio Railroad, he would have seen quite a bit of corn in the 1860s. The area of the prairie was also named the "Land of Egypt" due to its abundance of grain. There were "hundreds of bins filled with corn for the armies of the Confederacy. Each bin belonged to a farmer and it was his duty to keep it filled at fixed times."[50] Besides these feed cribs, the depots were laden with meal, bacon, white beans and hundreds of thousands of bushels of corn in the shuck. If one were able to be transported back to February 1864, he would look out from the tracks of the Mobile and Ohio Railroad and see thousands of acres of corn standing in the fields, brown and frozen.[51]

With all these supplies sitting in sheds beside the railroad, the Federal army hit pay dirt as far as forage was concerned. Its only problem was that it was unable to transport all of it, so the men burned almost all of it to keep it from falling into the hands of the Confederates. All these acres of supplies that had been saved to feed an army were bordered on the east by the Tombigbee River, the west by the Sakatonchee and the south by the Tibbee (formerly known as Oktibbeha) Creek. It was this area Forrest was trying to protect and keep out of the hands of the Federals. He knew they were heading down the Mobile and Ohio Railroad, and he knew they would lay their hands on the supplies waiting by the tracks. His objective was to keep them from lingering long enough to destroy much of the supplies and prevent them from tearing up the railroad. To do this, he had to get his troops into key strategic positions as quickly as possible to put continuous pressure on Sooy Smith to disallow him the privilege to stop for very long to do damage to the area.

Having been sent to Houston by Forrest to shadow Smith's movements south, Chalmers ran into problems getting to Houston. He had to face muddy roads and continuous rains. These conditions made traveling difficult even for horses. The roads were so bad that the artillery and wagons could not be pulled along the muddy roads. They kept getting mired down, which slowed the forward progress of the cavalry. Finally, Chalmers decided to move on to Houston without the wagons and artillery. He let them be brought up as soon as the teams could traverse the roads.

Chalmers arrived in Houston on February 16. From Houston, he cut across country to the southeast to the little community of Palo Alto. In Palo Alto, Chalmers entered an area where there was plenty of forage and subsistence. The little village had plenty of farms around it where grain was grown, as well as all other types of food that would feed an army. One of Chalmers's staff officers made this comment about Palo Alto: "The bountiful supplies of forage which the prairie furnished gladdened the hearts of our hungry horses, whose rations had been of the scantiest… when we came in sight of the first stack-yard, with its goodly array of huge fodder-ricks, and saw a little way off the teaming cribs, a shout of joy went up from the head of the column, which was continued down the whole line, as if we had indeed reached the promised land."[52]

As a means of contrast, there was an abundance of supplies stored along the railroad that Smith discovered when he had reached Egypt and other places south. His army had plenty to gorge itself on. The men also had plenty of forage for their horses. Joseph Karge reported that he had received orders from Smith to countermarch and form the extreme rear of the entire command. He was also ordered to shoot any man who fell out of the ranks. The reason for this was that the enemy shadowed the Federals on both flanks. Adjutant Pierson, according to Karge, brought in six large army wagons he found hidden in the swamps loaded with a lot of different goods and whiskey, all pulled by a team of six stout mules. The wagons and the stores within them were ordered burned. "The mules and drivers (colored), with about 100 of their friends, who all were anxious to be, joined to the train."[53]

Chalmers was fortunate to find the same type of abundances when he reached Palo Alto. It seems there was plenty of forage for both armies. When they left this area, both were well fed. Two differences existed between the two armies. One had to deal with the forage it could not take with it. The Federal army put to the torch everything it could not carry off. The Confederates in Palo Alto took what they needed but left the rest for the citizens of the area. The Federals took everything they could carry and burned the rest, leaving nothing behind for the citizens of the area. What a contrast between the two armies.

Smith moved his army south from Pontotoc to the west of Houston around the Houlka Swamp. He could not cross through the swamp because General Gholson's Partisan Rangers were defending the area. Smith did not want to get bogged down here, so he diverted his forward march to the east by heading toward Okolona. Once in Okolona, Smith turned south to follow the Mobile and Ohio Railroad.

General Forrest, after arriving in Grenada, turned his sights toward Starkville. He rapidly moved his command there, arriving on the eighteenth. Starkville was twenty-five miles west of Columbus, which was positioned along the Tombigbee River. Once Forrest arrived in Starkville, he set up a line of communication between Starkville and Palo Alto in order to keep in touch with Chalmers. Another strategic move made by Forrest was to send his brother, Colonel Jeffrey Forrest, toward Aberdeen "to harass and delay the enemy as much as practicable."[54]

On the eighteenth, Chalmers, along with his command, moved south from Palo Alto to Tampico, a crossroads about one mile north of the small community of Pheba. Here he found large supplies of forage. The next day, February 19, he joined Forrest at Starkville. While Chalmers was moving south to link up with General Forrest, Colonel Jeffrey Forrest was standing between the Federals and West Point. He was consistently striking them and then falling back but never engaging in an all-out battle.

Confederate Colonel Jeffrey Forrest. *Sons of Confederate Veterans Colonel Jeffrey Forrest Camp No. 323 and Brandon Beck.*

While Colonel Forrest was skirmishing with the Federals in the prairie, General Forrest had sent word to Bell's Brigade to have Colonel Barteau cross the Tombigbee at Columbus to the west side and ride north to intercept Smith, keeping him from crossing the river at Aberdeen and moving down the east side of the river to Columbus. Colonel Barteau discovered that Smith was moving en masse down to West Point, so he crossed to the west side of the Tombigbee at Waverley Landing to put himself between Smith and crossings along the Tombigbee that would enable Smith to get to the east side of the river.

Despite the Federal cavalry's route of travel, the men were watched and could be challenged by Forrest. As they began to move south, their direction of travel became apparent to Forrest, so he, in turn, adjusted some of his troops to oppose Smith's southerly movement, thus keeping him boxed in.

From these troop movements, we can assume that Forrest's plans were to stand between Sooy Smith's seven thousand men and Sherman's troops in Meridian. Forrest had no intentions of allowing Smith to break through to the south. As much as Forrest was prepared to fight, he was just as prepared to take the whole Union force without a fight by hemming it in, springing the trap and then capturing it. His plans to do this included guarding all the river crossings for the Tombigbee, Tibbee and Sakatonchee. At the confluence of the Tibbee, Sakatonchee and Line Creeks, a cul-de-sac was formed southwest of West Point where Forrest had hoped to trap the Federal cavalrymen, holding them until General Lee could arrive with his reinforcements.

Part II
Offense and Defense

War means fighting. To fight is the duty of a soldier. March swiftly, strike the foe with all your strength, and take away from him everything you can. Injure him in every possible way, and do it quickly.

–Stonewall Jackson to Dr. McQuire

Both sides went to great lengths to prepare their armies to face each other. The Federal army had to pull together enough cavalry to provide Sherman with a formidable force in Meridian. It also needed a considerably large force to take on Forrest if it happened to run into him.

General Forrest had his own problems building a new cavalry force large enough to face the enemy. He took great chances by slipping into west Tennessee under the noses of the Federal army to raise troops and gather supplies. His raid was a success; however, he had to get out of Tennessee with his new troops and supplies. So, under the nose of the Federal army, Forrest broke out of Tennessee, successfully escaping into Mississippi.

Federal Plans to Invade Mississippi

To better understand the northern phase of the Meridian Campaign, it is important to understand the preparations that the Federal cavalry made while still in Tennessee. It had to prepare its forces to move south into Mississippi to unite with Sherman in Meridian. The Federals had problems molding seven thousand troopers into a fighting force. Even though most of the men were in camps around Memphis, some had to come from as far north as Kentucky. Some had to journey from east Tennessee to Collierville, where they would all unite and proceed south.

Plans for this expedition began in January 1864 with a meeting between General Ulysses S. Grant and General William Tecumseh Sherman. Since Vicksburg had already been taken, the two generals wished to further subdivide Mississippi by sending an army across the state from Vicksburg to Meridian. If things worked as planned, they possibly would have proceeded into Alabama as far as Selma or even Mobile, although Sherman later said that his plans were to only go as far as Selma. To support this expedition, Grant and Sherman devised a plan for about seven thousand cavalry to leave Tennessee, travel the length of Mississippi along the railroad through the prairie and then to Meridian to link up with Sherman. They would have to travel more than two hundred miles to reach their rendezvous with Sherman. Grant selected William Sooy Smith to be commander of the cavalry, with Benjamin Grierson as his second in command. Grierson had plenty of experience with this route since he had taken it in 1863 in order to

Federal General Benjamin Grierson. *Library of Congress.*

interrupt railroad service between Meridian and Vicksburg by destroying the railroad at Newton Station.

Once this invasion plan had been devised, the next phase involved the tedious preparation of gathering troops. They had to be collected in one location for the beginning of the expedition. Smith's forces were assembled in Collierville, Tennessee. Sherman's forces were collected in Vicksburg for his part of the campaign to Meridian. Before the campaign began, Sherman sent a dispatch to all his troops reinforcing the importance of this mission. In order to reach Sherman by February 14, 1864, General William Sooy Smith had to leave Tennessee by February 1, 1864.

FEDERAL OFFENSE

Sherman left on time from Vicksburg to travel across the state to Meridian. On the other hand, Smith failed to get away from Collierville, Tennessee, on time. All of his cavalry had not arrived in Collierville by the departure date. On February 1, he had all his cavalry except a brigade, the 1st Brigade, commanded by Colonel George E. Waring Jr. Waring brought his troops from Columbus, Kentucky, down to join up with Smith. The weather had been a greater enemy to Waring's Brigade than the Confederates. He was slowed down by rain, mud, swollen creeks and rivers and ice due to cold weather. Waring described the challenges he faced moving his troops from camp in Columbus, Kentucky, to Colliersville, Tennessee, in the book *Whip and Spur*, written in 1897: "We lay in camp more than a week, ready to move, but awaiting orders. The country (a very wet one) was frozen hard and covered with snow. Our order to march and the thaw come together and the 22nd of January."[55]

Waring brought with him to Tennessee the following regiments: 4th Missouri (with a battery), 2nd New Jersey, 7th Indiana, 19th Pennsylvania and Frank Moore's Battalion of the 2nd Illinois. In all, he had about 2,500 men. Getting all these men and baggage across the creeks and through the mud was Waring's greatest challenge, but despite all the obstacles, Waring's force reached Collierville on February 8, 1864.

While Sooy Smith waited on Waring, he dispatched Colonel William L. McMillan of the 95th Ohio Infantry commanding the 1st Brigade of Infantry on an expedition from Memphis to Wyatt, Mississippi, to move within the general proximity of Panola. On February 6, McMillian's

Brigade moved southward to Hernando, spending the night there on February 7. They moved toward Coldwater on February 8, encountering Rebel pickets at the Coldwater Ferry. His troops drove back the Confederates by taking control of a ferryboat and crossing Coldwater Creek. During the evening of February 8, this Union force camped one and a half miles south of the Coldwater Depot. On the ninth, they moved two miles out on the Senatobia road, reaching the Hickahale stream. Unfortunately, the bridge gave way when they attempted to cross the stream, forcing them to spend several hours repairing the bridge before they could cross.

Advance units crossed the Hickahale, entering Senatobia and driving the Confederates from the town. On February 10, three bridges were destroyed that crossed the Hickahale after a sharp skirmish. By now, the brigade had received orders from Smith to return to Wyatt. When it arrived in Wyatt on the thirteenth, General Smith sent new orders for the men to meet him at Waterford. Once arriving in Waterford, McMillan received reports that Smith had moved on to New Albany. On the fifteenth, McMillan received orders from Smith to return to Memphis. The whole purpose of this brigade venturing into Mississippi was "to divert the attention of Forrest, Chalmers, and Lee, and allow General Smith to effect a crossing on the Tallahatchie."[56] By sending McMillan south while waiting on Waring, Smith created a diversion to throw Forrest off guard, making him think that the main force had chosen a different route than the one planned.

Waring's troops, upon arriving in Collierville, had to have all their horses reshod, fed and rested for the next leg of their journey. They were all broken down from their laborious trip from Columbus, Kentucky, to Collierville after trudging through the mud, ice and snow.

William Sooy Smith made an impression on George Waring, who shared his personal feelings about Smith in his book *Whip and Spur*, which was his first impression of the man he was to follow into Mississippi:

> *The chief in command was a young and handsome, but slightly nervous individual, who eschewed the vanities of uniform, and had about himself and his horse no evidence of his military character that could not be unbuckled and draped with his sword-belt in case of impending capture. He was vacillating in his orders, and a little anxious in his demeanor, but he had shown himself cool and clear-headed under fire, and seemed resolutely bent on the destruction of the last vestige of Forrest's troublesome army.*[57]

When Waring met Smith, he was not sure whether to follow Smith or not. The only credit he gave Smith was the fact he was "cool and clear-headed under fire." Practically speaking, this was the most important trait Smith needed to possess, for he was sure to run head-on into Forrest. He needed to be cool under fire because Forrest was surely going to give him all the battle he wanted and then some.

After being re-outfitted, with the horses fed and rested, the time arrived for Waring's Brigade, along with the rest of Smith's troops, to begin its part of the Meridian Campaign. The forces under Smith and Grierson making the trip into Mississippi included the following:

1ST BRIGADE (COLONEL GEORGE WARING):
- 2nd Illinois (five companies)
- 7th Indiana
- 4th Missouri
- 2nd New Jersey
- 19th Pennsylvania

2ND BRIGADE (LIEUTENANT COLONEL WILLIAM P. HEPBURN):
- 6th Illinois
- 7th Illinois
- 9th Illinois
- 1st Illinois Light Artillery Battery K
- 2nd Iowa

3RD BRIGADE (COLONEL LAFAYETTE MCCRILLIS):
- 3rd Illinois
- 72nd Indiana (mounted infantry)
- 5th Kentucky
- 2nd Tennessee
- 3rd Tennessee
- 4th Tennessee

UNATTACHED:
- 4th United States Cavalry

When the day came for Smith's columns to move out, the first group to leave Collierville was the 3rd Brigade, which left on February 10. The 3rd Brigade had 1,900 men. It crossed Coldwater Creek in Mississippi at

Quinn's Mill. Once across the Coldwater, the men camped at Raiford plantation, four miles east of Byhalia, where they waited for the main force led by General Sooy Smith.

RIDING WITH THE 1ST BRIGADE

The 1st Brigade—consisting of the 7th Indiana, 4th Missouri, 2nd New Jersey, 19th Pennsylvania Cavalry and five companies of the 2nd Illinois—left Collierville on February 11 around 2:00 p.m., camping at 6:00 p.m. on the farm of Colonel McLean, which was eleven miles out on the Moscow road. The road is out east, still in Tennessee, instead of south into Mississippi. They were sent to Moscow to meet a train from Memphis carrying forage "for night and morning and the remaining supplies which were required to fit out the brigade for the expedition."[58] Waring's report stated that the train did not arrive when it was scheduled to arrive. February 12 came, and the brigade was still waiting on the train. It finally arrived at around 10:30 a.m. on the twelfth. The supplies and forage were immediately issued. The brigade went on the march again at 2:00 p.m. and arrived in Hudsonville at 11:00 p.m. It traveled a total of twenty-three miles from where it met the train.[59] Once in Hudsonville, Waring received orders to proceed to Walker's Mills three miles east of Holly Springs. They stopped for one hour to rest both horses and men. The 1st Brigade then traveled all night, arriving on February 13 around 10:00 a.m. at Walker's Mills. The brigade had traveled sixteen miles from Hudsonville to Walker's Mills. After arriving, they waited for further orders from Sooy Smith.

Upon arriving at Walker's Mills, Waring sent a detachment of the 2nd Illinois Cavalry to Callahan's Mills to locate Sooy Smith. Waring's purpose in sending this detachment was to get orders concerning the brigade's next move south. When the detachment located Smith, he did not give the men any orders. Waring expressed his feelings about this incident:

> *February 14th, remained in camp at Walker's Mills expecting every movement orders to march. At 5 pm a messenger arrived from Colonel McCrillis at New Albany, communicating General Grierson's order for my brigade to proceed immediately to that point. This order instead of coming direct from General Grierson's headquarters, about 15 miles distant and first gone to New Albany and then come back to me. This delay caused*

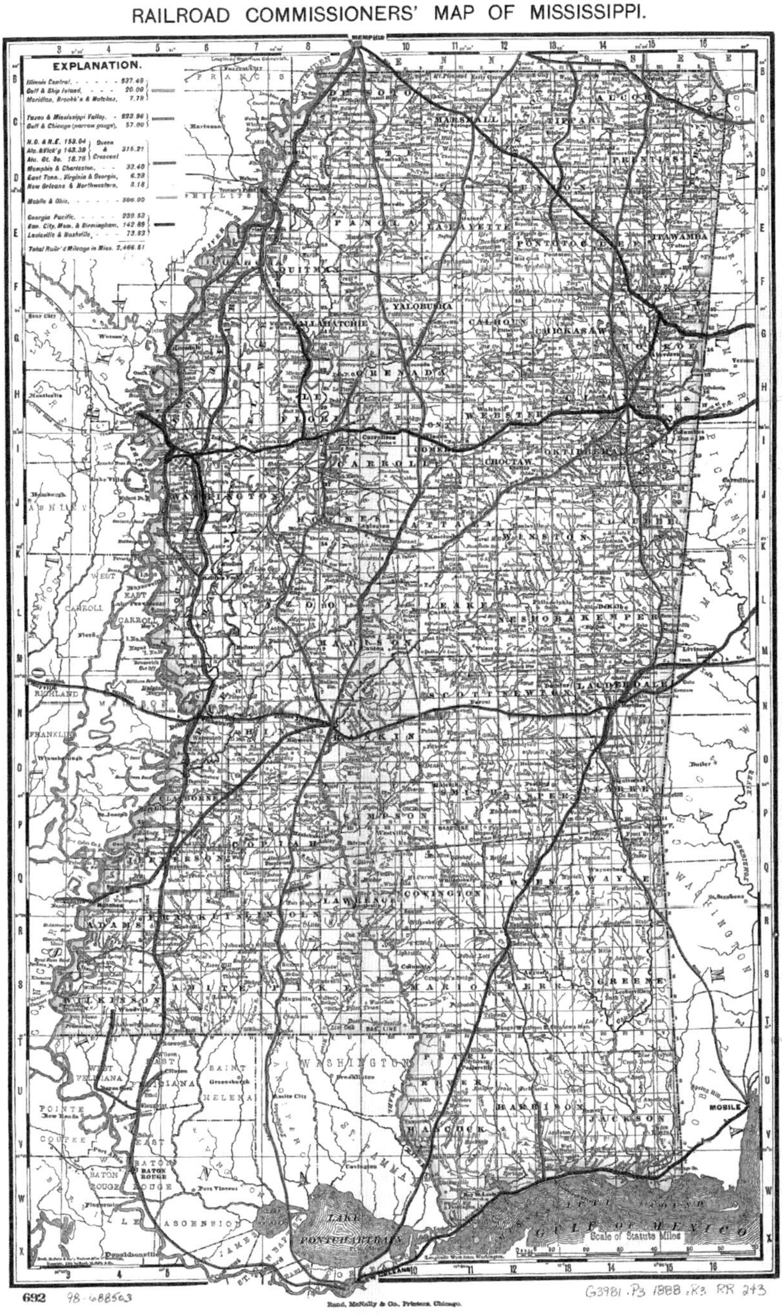

Railroad commissioner's map of Mississippi.

Above: A Federal cavalryman standing by his horse. *Library of Congress.*

Opposite: An 1864 railway county map of Mississippi.

> *more than a day's detention of my command. At the time when the order was received foraging parties were out, night was approaching, and it was raining heartily.*[60]

Leaving Walker's Mills at daylight on February 15, the brigade marched seven miles to Beck's Spring Ferry, located along the Tippah River, around 9:00 a.m. Upon arrival, the 1st Brigade found that the ferryboat was too small to carry the whole brigade across the river; the river was also impossible to cross because it was too high.

Joseph Karge, commander of the 2nd New Jersey Volunteer Cavalry, was leading one of the regiments that reached the Tippah River on February 15 around 1:00 p.m. Since there was no bridge present for them to use, they had to take time to build one, which took about six hours. The bridge

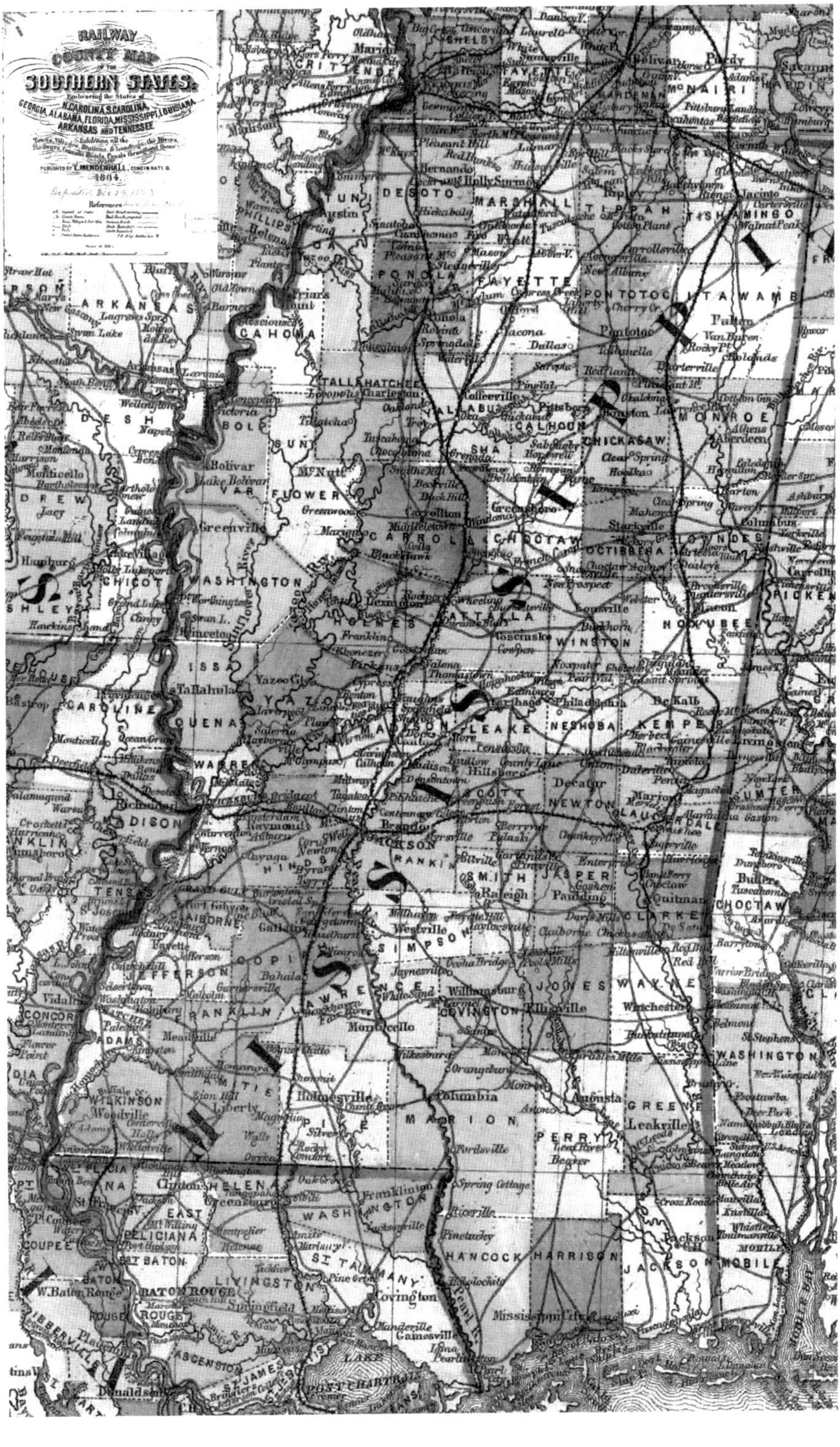
RAILWAY
COUNTY MAP
OF THE
SOUTHERN STATES,
Embracing the States of
N.CAROLINA, S.CAROLINA,
GEORGIA, ALABAMA, FLORIDA, MISSISSIPPI, LOUISIANA
ARKANSAS AND TENNESSEE
PUBLISHED BY E. MENDENHALL, CINCINNATI, O.
1864.
References

An improvised bridge across a creek. *Library of Congress.*

across the river was sixty-five feet long. By 3:00 p.m., they were ready to cross; however, the bridge had one flaw. Due to the rising river, the center of the bridge had been covered with water, hindering their crossing. Still they spent all night carefully crossing the bridge. Finally, by daylight, they had all crossed and camped on the other side.

The 1st Brigade broke camp the morning of February 16 and set out around 8:00 a.m. for New Albany. The roads were so bad due to the rains and muddy roads that six of their wagons had to be abandoned and destroyed. The 1st Brigade did not cross the Tallahatchie River until 8:00 p.m.

Before the whole brigade crossed the river, a detachment of the 19th Pennsylvania Cavalry was allowed to cross first and proceed to a point four miles south of New Albany on the Pontotoc road, where they encamped. All of the 19th Pennsylvania Cavalry, except for the detachment that camped south of New Albany, was ordered to return to Memphis, escorting prisoners and the sick. It was under the command of Lieutenant Colonel Hess. Passing through Holly Springs on the evening of the eighteenth, they reached Memphis with their prisoners around 4:00 p.m. on February 20.

Prisoners were turned over to the provost marshal, and the 19th Pennsylvania was ordered to Fort Pickering. The detachment of the 19th Pennsylvania under Major Holahan, which had traveled to New Albany, accompanied General Smith's expedition south.

When the one hundred men of the 19th Pennsylvania Cavalry crossed the Tallahatchie, they followed the Pontotoc road, reaching the camp of the 1st Brigade at about daybreak. Upon arriving, they discovered that the 1st Brigade had already begun moving out, so the one hundred men fell in the rear of the 7th Indiana. At about 8:00 a.m., the brigade reached the headquarters of Brigadier General Grierson, who was commanding the division. It had traveled about seven miles on the Pontotoc road. Upon reaching the headquarters of General Grierson, the men were ordered to proceed two or three miles farther ahead, where they received breakfast. Waring led his column two and a half miles farther south to the "farm of Parson Smith."[61] After one regiment had passed the headquarters of General Grierson, the rest of the brigade was ordered by General Smith to move to the side of the road so the 2nd and 3rd Brigades could pass and take the advance. Once the 2nd and 3rd Brigades had passed at about 2:00 p.m., the 1st Brigade fell in the rear of the column. They all marched to a

Federal column in twos (one of the ways that cavalry traveled). *Library of Congress.*

point nine miles south of Pontotoc, where they camped for the night. By the seventeenth, they had marched a total of twenty-five miles.

Boots and Saddle were sounded at 6:00 a.m. on February 18. The whole seven-thousand-man cavalry expedition got underway as one unit. The 2nd Brigade was given the honor of leading the column, although the brigade required two hours to move out. After taking the lead, the other two brigades fell in behind. For two hours, they trudged along until they received the order to halt. The road in front of the men had to be cleared of not only obstacles but also possible enemy (Confederate) snipers. After the road was cleared, the column moved out, once again passing through Red Land. It reached Houlka bottom east of Houston but was unable to cross due to General S.J. Gholson's 1st Mississippi Partisan Rangers blocking passage through the swamp. Instead of attempting to push through by brushing aside the Partisan Rangers, Smith chose to turn east toward Okolona. At about 4:00 p.m., the brigade arrived in Okolona, where General Smith ordered the 1st Brigade to proceed farther south to Egypt Station to ascertain a suitable campsite. Devastation against Southern property began at this time. The 1st Brigade received an order by General Smith to "destroy such property along the line of the railroad as might belong to the rebel government and… destroy the railroad itself."[62]

The head of the column receive fire from twenty to thirty Confederate soldiers when it had advanced about two miles from Okolona. During the night, the 19th Pennsylvania and the Pioneer Corps were sent ahead to Egypt Station, eight miles south of Okolona, to destroy railroad and government supplies.

By daybreak on February 19, the 1st Brigade rode to Egypt Station except for one battalion of the 7th Indiana Cavalry, which remained in Okolona and joined the brigade later. Major Prosser of the 2nd Tennessee Cavalry (USA) was ordered to move with two hundred men at 5:30 a.m. toward the southwest in the direction of Houston, while the 3rd Brigade continued south.

Major Prosser and his men ran into about twenty-five or thirty men from a well-mounted Confederate scouting party two or three miles from camp. Having good mounts aided the Confederates' escape, except they had to leave behind their pack mules. After adventuring one and a half miles farther into Rebel territory, Prosser and his men drove in pickets at the fork of the Pontotoc, Okolona and Houston roads. Five miles closer to Houston, they turned left on the Buena Vista road. Riding six miles farther south, they ran into pickets who were a part of General S.J. Gholson's 1st

Mississippi Partisan Rangers. Gholson's whole brigade had camped here but had already moved off in the direction of West Point, except for four hundred men and General Gholson himself. Gholson was routed from his camp and pursued by Prosser's men to within two miles of West Point.

When the Federal column arrived at Egypt Station at about 9:00 a.m., it immediately began destroying government property around the station. A.J. Holahan, major of the 19th Pennsylvania Cavalry, received orders from Colonel Waring to "destroy the railroad and stores at that point."[63] Holahan described the work his men performed, destroying everything of value to the Confederates at Egypt Station:

> *I immediately threw out a sufficient force to picket the roads; then destroyed the telegraph and fell to work at the railroad. Great difficulty was experienced in making rapid progress in the destruction of the road* [railroad] *for want of proper tools, but shortly after the tools of the road*

Federal troop destruction of the railroad. *Library of Congress.*

were discovered in a house some distance from the station these were at once brought into requisition, and by 9 am some 300 yards of the road were effectually destroyed, the rails torn up and bent, while large fires were built over the track, which I was unable, for want of time, to tear up. At 9:30 am Colonel Waring came up and directed me to fire all the stores found in the place; then rejoin the brigade and act as rear guard.[64]

The 19th Pennsylvania Cavalry captured 100,000 bushels of corn, 5,000 bushels of meal and bran, five sacks of salt, four boxes of tobacco, one hundred muskets and five thousand grain bags, as well as the mail at Egypt Station. They burned cornmeal, muskets and sacks of salt along with the depot, a workshop and a storehouse. Afterward, resuming their march on the Aberdeen road, they began receiving many slaves from area plantations. They were loaded down with the great amount of contraband supplies stolen from the plantation. These slaves attached themselves to the Federal column. Concerning the slaves who had attached themselves to Smith's column, Smith wrote about them in his after-battle report:

About 3,000 able-bodied negroes had taken refuge with us, mounted on as many horses and mules that they had brought in with them. We had in addition to this about 700 pack-mules, and all these incumbrances had to

Column of slaves leaving the plantation. *Library of Congress.*

> *be strongly guarded against the flank attacks that were constantly threatened. This absorbed about 2,000 of my available force. There remained a little less than 5,000 men who could be thrown into action.*[65]

Meeting the rest of the brigade after it had taken a wrong turn, the 19th Pennsylvania Cavalry took the lead of brigade. Finally, at dark, they all reached Prairie Station.

PRAIRIE STATION

The 4th Tennessee Cavalry (USA), commanded by Lieutenant Colonel Jacob M. Thornburgh, was ordered to proceed to the railroad at Prairie Station to tear up the tracks and destroy all the property belonging to the Confederates. He found four freight cars loaded with flour and meal, as well as twenty-eight pens of corn. The depot was also filled with corn. They burned all of these supplies. The 4th Tennessee tore up tracks by heating the rails with fire provided by burning crossties. They then bent the red-hot rails around poles or trees, creating what Confederates called "Sherman neckties." Afterward, they returned to the brigade heading for West Point.

Colonel W.P. Hepburn, commander of the 2nd Brigade, moved his entire command in the direction of West Point on the morning of February 20. The 2nd Iowa was in advance of the brigade. The 6th Illinois was on the left flank on the railroad, which they destroyed. They also burned large quantities of corn belonging to the Confederacy. When they approached Loohatten Station (Muldon), Colonel Starr reported "the enemy in force at a point about 6 miles north of West Point."[66] An advance patrol, about seventeen men of Company K, 2nd Iowa Cavalry, under the command of Lieutenant Bandy, came upon a Confederate force that outnumbered Company K. Bandy charged the enemy, putting them to flight and capturing several prisoners. On the morning of February 20, at 9:00 a.m., the 1st Brigade left Prairie Station for West Point.

NORTH OF WEST POINT

Falling in behind the 2nd Brigade, the 1st Brigade under Colonel Waring arrived in West Point at about 3:00 p.m. in excellent condition. The 3rd Brigade marched to within two and a half miles of West Point and remained there until the twenty-first.

The advance of the 2nd Iowa was checked one and a half miles north of West Point, where a Confederate force under the command of Colonel Jeffrey Forrest was waiting. The Confederates were hidden in a stand of timber and behind fences; from these positions, they attacked the 2nd Iowa, stopping its forward progress. When the 2nd Iowa received reinforcements from the rest of the brigade, the Confederates were driven back. The 2nd Iowa occupied West Point one hour later, and the whole brigade encamped near West Point the night of the twentieth. In the skirmish north of town, the 2nd Iowa lost Lieutenant Dwire. Four men also received wounds in the skirmish.

Commanding the 2nd Iowa, Major Datus Coon reported that he had "good opportunities for gathering information of the location and numbers of Forrest's command, and had at no time placed the force at the Sakatonchee bridge above 2,000 men and this force without artillery."[67]

When the Federals reached West Point, they received reports that the three Forrests (general, colonel and captain) had just left town and passed west across the Sakatonchee River three miles west of West Point. The Federals did not know Colonel Jeffrey Forrest and Captain William Forrest (a third Forrest brother) were actually in the area. General Forrest was the

Cavalry at a charge. *Library of Congress.*

only one who had returned to his headquarters in Starkville. He was not in the immediate area when the Federals arrived at West Point.

What was the Confederate army doing while General Smith was arriving with his cavalry in West Point? Where were the Confederates? What were their positions?

CONFEDERATE DEFENSES

While Sooy Smith was marching his forces south as quickly as he could, Sherman had already arrived in Meridian on February 14. Smith did not leave Collierville, Tennessee, until February 11. He was already far behind schedule. In comparison to Sherman's march across the state, Smith faced many more hindrances. He had to contend with muddy roads and swollen creeks. Besides these natural obstacles, there was the constant threat of Forrest. Smith never knew when Forrest was going to show up with his army and attack him. Smith knew that Forrest could strike him from any direction and at any point. He constantly had to be diligent in his preparation to face Forrest.

Sherman's army did not face any real threats as it moved east toward Meridian from Vicksburg. What opposition he did face was swept aside by his massive Federal forces. Before reaching Meridian, General Leonidas Polk pulled his forces out of Meridian across the Tombigbee River toward Demopolis, Alabama.

Generals Stephen D. Lee and Wirt Adams were left in central Mississippi with their cavalry to face Sherman. They did not have enough men to engage in a head-to-head fight with Sherman. All they could do was carry on guerrilla warfare by striking at Sherman's forces and then retreating to a place where they could safely pick another fight.

SHADOWING THE ENEMY

The Confederacy's only hope in Mississippi to destroy Sherman's plan rested with General Forrest's attempts in north Mississippi to interfere with Sooy Smith's endeavor to join his forces with Sherman's in Meridian. Even though Smith had a far superior army than Forrest's, Forrest had the advantage. He knew the country better than Smith from Tennessee south to West Point. Forrest even had men serving with him whose homes were in West Point. Forrest had a superb system of scouts scattered all over north Mississippi to keep a close watch on Sooy Smith's operations. They kept Forrest well informed of all Federal troop movements. To a certain extent, the element of surprise was in Forrest's favor the whole time the Federal army was moving to West Point.

Following his recruiting activities in west Tennessee, Forrest returned to Mississippi, where he began preparing for a possibly long engagement. He organized his new recruits into a fighting force. His forces were then sent to strategic sites across north Mississippi to cover bridge crossings, ferries and other river crossings that could be utilized by the Federal army. He had patrols of cavalry scouting the countryside watching for possible Federal troop movements.

Forrest had moved part of his forces from Panola and Como to Grenada. On February 14, he sent a dispatch to General Polk describing his actions up to that point: "I have skirmished with the enemy from Panola to [the] mouth of Tippah River. Their forces are moving to my right, crossing Tippah today 10 miles above its mouth on the road to New Albany. I am of opinion the larger portion of their forces will move via Pontotoc to Houston or Okolona and thence southward."[68]

Forrest, along with his escort company, hastily moved south. He had other forces that accompanied him south as well. They were trying to strategically position themselves between Smith and Meridian. The forces with Forrest were not the only ones moving south, though. Other troops in Forrest's command hurried to place themselves in positions to stand between Smith and Meridian.

During the evening of February 14, General Forrest sent his brother, Colonel Jeffrey Forrest, and Brigadier General Chalmers to move their brigades toward Houston to oppose any possible advance in that direction by Smith. In the same dispatch Forrest wrote on the evening of February 14 from Grenada, he said, "I have ordered all the balance of my forces to concentrate here, and will follow to West Point with all my forces tomorrow. Watch your right wing closely, and have General Lee's forces in position to cooperate with me. In the event the enemy proves to strong for me I shall fall back in the enemy's front toward Meridian, in case I am forced to fall back at all."[69]

The same afternoon, Colonel Forrest's brigade, with a battery of artillery, left Grenada at about 2:00 p.m. for West Point. Brigadier General Chalmers, along with Colonel McCulloch's brigade and a battery of mountain howitzers, left Oxford at 4:00 p.m. heading for West Point. Richardson's and Bell's brigades, along with two batteries, left on February 15 at about 4:00 p.m. following Colonel Forrest for West Point.[70]

PREPARING TO MAKE A STAND

"Think I can make West Point by morning of 19th,"[71] wrote Forrest. He chose to make a stand in West Point against Smith's cavalry. Forrest, knowing about the three bodies of water around West Point, utilized them to set a trap for Smith. The Tombigbee River was on the east, Tibbee Creek on the south and Sakatonchee Creek on the west. Each of these bodies of water had crossings that could be used by the Federals as well as the Confederates. All three together provided a strategic obstacle for Smith. They created a partial box within which Forrest could trap Smith. By placing his forces at each crossing, the Union cavalry would have to fight to get across. If they did attempt to cross at any of these locations, Forrest's plan was to shut the door to the trap. He would then either capture them or try to decimate Smith's forces. Due to his horse sense, Forrest understood what it took to defeat his enemy. While Smith and his cavalry were steadily moving south, Forrest's troops were constantly repositioning themselves to shadow Smith's movements, as well as challenge him when the odds appeared in favor of the Confederates.

General S.J. Gholson, commander of the 1st Mississippi Partisan Rangers, sent a dispatch to General Daniel Ruggles, informing him of Federal troop movements. The dispatch stated that his scouts placed the enemy "this side of New Albany coming down the country, whether on this road or by Okolona."[72] Gholson was in Red Land on February 15, 1864. Red Land was located in the southwest corner of Pontotoc County, northwest of Houston.

On the evening of February 16, 1864, Jeffrey Forrest and his 4th Brigade were encamped on the Judge Calvert farm in the northwest part of Clay County (then part of Chickasaw County) in Palo Alto. Colonel Forrest sent a dispatch to General Ruggles commenting on the dispatch he saw from General Gholson. He also reported on the condition of his forces:

> *General: When I reached this place on my way to West Point I saw dispatch from General Gholson stating that the enemy was this side of New Albany, coming this way. I will remain here until I hear from you, or until I ascertain more of the enemy. I have asked General Gholson to keep me posted. My horses are very tired. I saw a scout going out this morning from West Point. Duff's Battalion and Morton's battery went a road south of this. I have sent after them to come here. I am about 16 miles from West Point on Houston road* [Houston road ran through Palo Alto]. *I will put a courier post between here and West Point. I will keep courier line to Houston and a scout also there. I will need some ammunition and will send to West Point for it.*[73]

When General Forrest arrived in Starkville during the afternoon of February 18, he immediately set up his headquarters there. After arriving, he sent a dispatch to General S.D. Lee informing him that his forces were lacking sufficient ammunition to oppose the Federal army. He did not have more than forty rounds of cartridges to the man. Besides not having enough ammo, his artillery horses were jaded. They had been pulling artillery through mud and muck all day. Forrest also requested from General Lee some small-arms ammunition, preferably .54 calibers for his men.[74]

Determined to fight Sooy Smith, Forrest prepared for that eventuality somewhere around West Point. He had already experienced several skirmishes with Smith while moving south. Lee was informed by Forrest on

February 18 that all his men were posted in strategic positions in the area to oppose Smith's Federals. Forrest wrote to Lee, "Have three brigades here, with all my artillery. McCulloch's brigade is 25 miles north of this."[75]

Forrest's troops were positioned from the Sakatonchee Creek three miles west of West Point to the Tombigbee east of West Point. The area south of West Point down to the Tibbee community and Tibbee Creek and west to the confluence of Sakatonchee and Line Creek was covered. General S.J. Gholson with his Partisan Rangers covered the area north of Palo Alto all the way to Houlka Swamp in case Smith attempted to turn west and then south.

A Tactical Dance

We have two challengers playing chess. Each makes a move on the chessboard trying to either maneuver forward to the opposite side or check the movement of the opponent. Both sides try to keep their king from getting checked. The big question for Forrest was what direction was Sooy Smith going to take with his cavalry to attempt a move south. For Sooy Smith, his big question was where exactly Forrest was, as well as how many men he had to oppose him.

For several days, Forrest had been in the saddle, steadily journeying south from the northwest corner of Mississippi to Starkville. During this time, he had constantly shadowed the movements of the Union army. He did not have time to take care of behemoth tasks like the provision of ammunition. Arriving in Starkville ahead of the Union army, Forrest had time to take care of his troops by attempting to acquire weapons, ammunition and accoutrements. While in Starkville, Forrest gave his horses time to rest, especially those pulling artillery. He learned that "General Clark, or Governor Clark, has some ammunition, caliber 54."[76] His sent a question to Governor Clark: "[C]annot some of it—say 50,000 rounds—be sent up on hand cars to Artesia? I can get along with that amount, having plenty for all other arms except the Austrian rifles and Sharps rifles."[77] The Sharps used a .52-caliber bullet, and the Austrians used a .54-caliber bullet. Every man possible needed to be properly outfitted in order to take on Sooy Smith's seven-thousand-man army.

Reports reached Forrest on the nineteenth, noting the enemy was reported at Okolona but that there was some uncertainty as to what Smith's route was going to be. They did not know which direction he intended to follow. Forrest's fear was that Smith might try to cross the Tombigbee and head south on the east side of the river. To counter Smith, Bell's Brigade was ordered to Columbus, and Forrest also "dispatched General Ruggles to use all his effective forces to prevent them [Union army] from doing so."[78] Besides transferring Bell's Brigade to Columbus, he ordered Brigadier General Chalmers, who was commanding a division, to send Colonel Forrest's brigade to Aberdeen or "in that direction, to meet and ascertain the movements of the enemy."[79] McCulloch's brigade of Chalmers's division was ordered to move out to West Point. Richardson was to remain in Starkville with the dismounted men of the command to protect the wagon train.

Scouts were also sent out in the direction of Houston to warn Forrest in case Smith decided to split his forces, sending part of them south through Houston, which would place them in Forrest's rear. Any movement by Smith's forces toward Houston would have been detected by Forrest's scouts. The possibility of Smith taking this route was great since he was accompanied by General Benjamin Grierson, his second in command, who had followed this route when commanding an expedition in 1863 toward the railhead at Newton Station. Grierson was very familiar with this route. If Smith had chosen to follow this route with Grierson in the lead, it would have placed him in Forrest's rear. Forrest's forces were placed in positions around the area to keep Smith bottled in. The plan was to channel Smith's forces between his men into a cul-de-sac formed by the three creeks south of West Point and the Tombigbee east of West Point. If Smith fell for the bait, it would be a tactical error, allowing him to be trapped between three wings of Forrest's army.

General Smith's objective, as he was attempting to link up with Sherman in Meridian, was to reach the fertile prairie region. By February 19, his troops had entered this area. It was teeming with grains, cotton and military equipment. Besides the railroad at Egypt Station, there were warehouses filled with supplies. Smith's troops took what they needed and destroyed the rest. They tore up the railroads so they could not be used again.

The 7th Tennessee Cavalry under Colonel Jeffrey Forrest met the Union forces between Aberdeen and Egypt Station. "The regiment skirmished lightly as they were slowly pressed back toward West Point."[80] While the 7th Tennessee was heavily engaged in the front, it sent a regiment out on the flank of the enemy to attempt getting to his rear. This regiment was discovered. The men had to fall back rapidly. When they did, the regiment was forced to run the gauntlet of a brigade formation of the enemy on the roadside.[81]

In the meantime, in a dispatch written on February 20, 1864, Colonel C.G. Armistead described his efforts to unite with Colonel Forrest: "I...

learned from the scouts that Colonel Forrest was moving in the direction of the enemy on the West Point and Aberdeen road. I then changed my course so as to intercept Colonel Forrest, which I did at Payne's Chapel, 8 or 10 miles from Aberdeen."[82]

Colonel Forrest, along with four hundred men of his brigade, moved toward Aberdeen, where he encountered enemy pickets whom he routed and drove back into Aberdeen. Afterward, Jeffrey Forrest fell back with his men to Payne's Chapel, where they remained until 2:00 a.m. Scouts were dispatched in all directions to ascertain the location of the enemy. They reported back that the enemy was concentrated in Aberdeen. Residents of Aberdeen reported to Confederate scouts that the enemy force had left Aberdeen for Houston the evening of the nineteenth. They headed in that direction to join with the rest of Smith's forces around Prairie Station. Discovering the enemy's direction of travel, Colonel Forrest worked around the enemy's left and rear to continuously execute hit-and-run attacks to slow down the Union forces and draw them to West Point. He did not want to engage in an all-out battle. All he wanted to do was commit a series of skirmishes to draw Smith's army toward West Point. He, as well as the Union army, experienced some difficulty with the roads since this was the rainy season and all the streams were out of their banks.[83]

While Colonel Forrest was playing his cat-and mouse game of making a stand between the Federals and West Point and then falling back, General Forrest was moving his men to the Sakatonchee to assist Chalmers and his remaining brigade. Forrest took with him Richardson's brigade along with two batteries of artillery and joined Colonel Forrest three miles north of West Point.

A DEFENSIVE STAND

Noticing the immense strength of the forces opposing him, General Forrest decided to fall back south of Sakatonchee Creek, behind Ellis Bridge, three miles west of West Point. Forrest made the decision to fall back because he did not want to engage the enemy until he had received reinforcements from General S.D. Lee. All Forrest was interested in doing was drawing the enemy back into the cul-de-sac on the West Point to Starkville road south of town and attack them there.[84] By holding the ground west of Ellis Bridge, Forrest wanted to "delay a general engagement as long as

Old West Point road south of West Point taken by Federal troops. *Photo by John W. McBryde.*

possible."[85] He let Jeffrey Forrest pull the enemy through West Point and down the road to the cul-de-sac.

On the evening of February 20, a courier reported to Forrest that a detachment of the 4th U.S. Regulars had crossed Sakatonchee eight miles north of Ellis Bridge around Siloam. They had destroyed mills and stolen horses and slaves. Forrest, with five companies of Faulkner's regiment and his escort company, rode up the creek to Siloam in order to put a stop to the 4th U.S. Regulars' activities. When Forrest arrived, he captured twenty-two privates and a lieutenant. While there, Forrest gave the order to burn the bridge to keep any more of Smith's forces from attempting to cross Sakatonchee. Once Forrest and his men had taken care of this problem, they returned to Ellis Bridge, where they had to decide what to do with their prisoners.

Growing up in the Siloam community, I used to hear the story told by my elders of how Forrest got rid of the prisoners who tried to cross at Siloam. They told how Forrest's men took these prisoners to Harmon Lake, which is less than one mile from Ellis Bridge.

They tied their hands behind their backs and marched them downstream to Harmon Lake, which was quite deep at the time. When it became obvious that they were being sent to a watery grave, one handsome young prisoner pleaded for his life; he told his captors that he had a wife and small children at home who needed him. But his pleas were in vain. The young man and the rest of the prisoners were marched forward until the waters closed over their heads.[86] I have never heard anything to rebuke this story. The official reports from General Forrest only say that they took some prisoners at Siloam.

Forrest defended his reason for holding Ellis Bridge in his after-battle report: "This bridge I determined, if possible, to defend and preserve, because it was necessary in the event we could drive back the enemy to use it in advancing on them; and had I allowed the enemy to cross it and then succeeded in driving them back they would have burned it behind them, rendering pursuit impossible without heading the stream."[87]

Accounts of Forrest's activities at Ellis Bridge were related in the *Southern Historical Society Papers* in 1879. Chalmers related the activities of February 20, 1864:

> *On the 20th Bell's Brigade was sent to keep on the flank of the enemy and cover Columbus, and McCulloch and Richardson moved up to support Jeff Forrest, and all fell back, slowly skirmishing to West Point. A telegram received here announced that General S.D. Lee with brigades, would be with us early on the 22nd, and Forest retired behind Suquatoncha Creek, of steep banks and miry bottom, and over which there were but few bridges, easily defended. This was a perfectly safe position, where he could easily hold the enemy in check until he could arrive. Smith was in a complete cul-de-sac, formed by the Suquatoncha on his right, the Tibbee before him, and the Tombigbee on his left and Lee and Forrest united could have cross Suquatoncha behind him and capture his command.*[88]

Once all of Forrest's command was positioned to take on Sooy Smith, the men spent the night in their assigned positions, looking at the glowing sky north of West Point—the country was "illuminated by burning homesteads, cotton gins, granaries, and stack-yards."[89] These fires infuriated the Confederates to the point that they were spoiling for a fight. They wanted badly to "punish such an unmanly method of warfare."[90] Not all of the Confederates were sitting idly by watching that orange glow, however. Colonel Jeffrey Forrest was on the north side of the Sakatonchee Creek and Ellis Bridge, with his men stationed about half a mile from the bridge. They busied themselves "throwing up temporary breastworks of rails and logs."[91]

A fight was sure to come, but no one, including Colonel Forrest, General Forrest or Brigadier General Chalmers, knew when it would come. They expected Sooy Smith to force a crossing at Ellis Bridge. By the evening of February 20, Forrest had all his troops positioned to engage Smith if a fight did occur. They were camped along the Sakatonchee. General William Sooy Smith's troops (whom a local matron called "those dreaded wretches")[92] were camped around the Westbrook place on the north side of town on the evening of February 20, 1864. The stage was set for a fight.

Part III
The Battle

The quality of decision is like the well-timed swoop of a falcon which enables it to strike and destroy its victim.

–Sun Tzu

Skirmishing continued as the Federals moved south through the Prairie toward West Point. Confederate forces under Jeffrey Forrest fell back toward the southwest through West Point, traveling down the Starkville road toward the Tibbee Creek crossing after they determined to draw the army of Sooy Smith into the bottom. Their objective was to lure Smith into a trap whereupon Forrest could close in around the Federal cavalry, preventing their escape. When Smith did arrive early in West Point on February 20, he encountered Jeffrey Forrest's brigade, which retreated toward the southwest as it attempted to draw Smith into "a three-sided box, formed by the Tombigbee River on the east, and, on the south and west, the muddy valleys of Oktibbeha and Sakatonchee creeks."[93] Smith later commented that he decided "to move back and draw the enemy after me that I might select my own positions and fight with the advantages in our favor."[94] Explaining why he decided not to pursue Jeffrey Forrest down the West Point–Starkville road, he said that "all the state troops that could be assembled from every quarter were drawn together at my front to hold the Oktibbeha against me, while a heavy force was seen moving to my rear…Under the circumstances, I determined not to move my encumbered command into the trap set for me by the rebels."[95] Instead, Smith pulled back to West Point to spend the night there.

Site where the Westbrook place stood, where Smith and Grierson spent the night in West Point. *Photo by John W. McBryde.*

By nightfall, Federal forces had settled down around West Point, making their camps along the old Aberdeen-Starkville road (Old West Point road) on the western outskirts of the town. Many camped at the old Wooten place west of this road. Small fires could be seen flickering all over the western edge of town by local citizens. Far off to the north of town, the skyline was illuminated by a large orange-red glow from fires emanating from burning plantations, grain bins, cotton warehouses and other plantation outbuildings. Those not set fire by the Federal forces moving through the area were set by rampaging slaves before they left the plantations to attach themselves to the Federal army.

General Smith, on the evening of February 20, set up headquarters in a house on the outskirts of town beside the road entering West Point from the north. The house was located on the corner of Highway 45 North and Dunlap road. It is no longer there, for it was torn down years ago. Smith was sick when he arrived in West Point. It appears he had a lot of apprehension about continuing his mission south to link up with Sherman. Smith felt ill from the stress of the mission and suffered terribly at times from arthritis. He believed that Forrest had set a trap for him south of town. He called an officer's council at midnight at his headquarters. Grierson described

Slaves with loaded wagon fleeing the South. *Library of Congress.*

Smith in his report as "absolutely sick and unable to command in such an emergency."[96] Smith believed that Sherman had already reached Meridian and was on his way back to Vicksburg. He felt that Forrest and Stephen D. Lee would destroy his command if he continued south. The best part of valor, according to Smith, was to return to Tennessee with his command intact. Not sure how his command would respond under fire, Smith felt that he had only one brigade that showed any promise in a fight. So, he believed, the best thing for him to do was to return to his base in Tennessee.

Besides Smith's arriving late in Meridian, his own health and the probability that two of his brigades would not give their all when tested under fire, he had another problem: maneuvering in battle. Nearly three thousand contraband items—composed of slaves with baggage, horses and mules—had attached themselves to his command.

When Smith suggested that they return to their home base in Collierville, Tennessee, his cavalry commanders refused to retreat, for they wanted to proceed to Meridian. Smith explained to them that he was too sick to continue this mission. Command was turned over to Grierson. When asked by Smith what he planned to do, Grierson informed Smith that he proposed to complete

General Benjamin Grierson and staff. *Library of Congress.*

their mission. Smith responded that this would not work since General Lee was in front of them with his force, waiting to strike if they continued south. Furthermore, Forrest was out there waiting to destroy him. Miraculously, Smith recovered from his sick spell well enough to reclaim command from Grierson. He then ordered a countermarch to Memphis.[97]

When the Federal forces arrived in West Point, the lieutenant colonel of the 6th Illinois Cavalry, M.H. Starr, reported that there was cause for concern east of the town along the Columbus road. He sent Captain Blackburn and Company A, 9th Illinois Cavalry, along with Captain M.L. Webster and one company of the 7th Illinois Cavalry out on the West Point–Columbus road. They ran into "a considerable force of the enemy's [Confederate] cavalry; a vigorous attack made by the companies of Captains Webster and Blackburn dispersed them completely."[98] Today, this road runs southeast of West Point to the Tombigbee River at Waverley Mansion.

FINAL PREPARATIONS FOR BATTLE

Confederate troops had pulled back to the west side of Sakatonchee Creek three miles west of town, except for those throwing up temporary breastworks of trees, fence rails and anything else they could scare up to provide protection from Federal bullets. These breastworks were built north of Ellis Bridge along the road to the bridge. Once the Confederate troops took cover behind their breastworks, their objective was to protect the bridge from capture since it was a strategic structure in this campaign. If it fell into enemy hands, the Federals would gain an open road to Meridian.

While all the work to fortify the bridge was still going on, the rest of the troopers were bivouacking for the evening west of the bridge on a hill across

A bridge similar to what Ellis Bridge would have looked like. *Library of Congress.*

the bottom. Small campfires could be seen where Forrest's army was settling down for the evening. These troops anticipated a fight the next day.[99]

General Forrest had returned to Starkville after killing or capturing men of a detachment of the 4th U.S. Regulars. While awaiting the arrival of General S.D. Lee with reinforcements, Forrest received a dispatch from Lee announcing that he, along with three brigades, "would be with us early on the 22nd."[100] Hoping to hold out until Lee's arrival, Forrest "placed his men behind Sakatonchee Creek, of steep banks and miry bottom and over which there were but few bridges."[101]

Colonel Jeffrey Forrest's forces were still building breastworks while the rest of the army was bivouacked for the night. This place was described by T.M. Moseley of the 8th Mississippi Cavalry, attached to Forrest's command. Moseley drew a map in 1926 of the battlefield, with diagrams showing where the troops were located.[102]

Colonel Forrest's men remained on the east side of the bridge, throwing up "breastworks of rails and logs for the protection of his men and to strengthen his position for the fight which he anticipated would take place in the ensuing morning."[103] The Confederates had to be ready to defend the bridge.

FEDERAL ADVANCE

Sunday morning, February 21, finally arrived. The Confederate vedettes (mounted soldiers on picket or guard duty)[104] and pickets (soldiers on guard along with others)[105] were on duty well out ahead of their main line to watch for enemy movements in their direction. A picket's duty was to warn his line of an enemy approaching in order to prevent a surprise attack. Both the vedettes and pickets were forced to retreat to the main Confederate lines in front of the creek since a Federal brigade was on the move west. When the vedettes and pickets arrived at the bridge, they reported to Colonel Jeffrey Forrest that the enemy troops were heading their way.[106] In response to these reports, General Chalmers dismounted his division on the west side of the creek, and Jeffrey Forrest's brigade took its position on the east side of the creek to oppose the enemy when they appeared.

McCulloch had been ordered to move his brigade to the west side of the bridge and support Colonel Forrest in case his forces had to retreat to the west side of the creek. Colonel Richardson was with his forces in Starkville protecting the wagons and artillery. He received a dispatch ordering him to move up all of his forces to the bridge, across Line Creek, eight miles from Starkville and four miles in Forrest's rear. Colonel Barteau was ordered to move Bell's Brigade across the Tombigbee from the east side of the river to the west side at Waverley Landing to stay on General Smith's right flank and gain Smith's rear if possible.[107] Colonel Barteau was in command of this brigade for the moment because Colonel Tyree Bell, the regular commander, was sick. Colonel Neely moved his brigade to guard the ferries and fords across Tibbee Creek from the mouth of Line Creek to Tibbee Station. Finally, General Gholson was dispatched with his state forces, commonly known in Mississippi as Partisan Rangers, to Palo Alto to watch movements of the enemy in the direction of Houston.

General Sooy Smith became deeply concerned about the locations of Forrest's troops. After the campaign, Smith expressed his concerns in an after-battle report:

> *The enemy was in a position in my front and on my flanks which afforded him every advantage. The ground was so obstructed as to make it absolutely necessary that we should fight dismounted, and for this kind of fighting the enemy armed with Enfield and Austria rifles, was better prepared than our force, armed mainly with carbines. There was but one of my brigades that I could rely upon with full confidence. The conduct of the other two on the march had been such as to indicate such a lack of discipline as to create in my mind the most serious apprehensions as to what would be their conduct in action. Any reverse to my command, situated as it was, would have been fatal.*[108]

From General Smith's reports, we can ascertain that he appeared to have questioned his abilities and that of his troops to carry out their mission. In fact, by the time Smith reached West Point, he had a lot of doubt as to whether he could continue the mission at all. Smith had received reports from captured Confederates that Forrest had more than ten thousand men scattered around the area to entrap Smith. What Smith did not know was that Forrest had allowed these men to be captured so they could share erroneous information with Smith about the strength of his forces. Forrest was using a new type of psychological warfare to place doubt in the minds of his enemy. Due to this false information, Smith made the decision to return his command to Tennessee. Smith justified his actions by spelling out in his report the damage his forces had inflicted on the prairie while marching to West Point:

> *We had destroyed 2,000,000 bushels of corn, 2,000 bales of Confederate cotton, and 30 miles of railroad. We had captured about 200 prisoners, and 3,000 horses and mules, and rescued as many negroes, well fitted for our service. I, therefore, determined to move back and draw the enemy after me, that I might select my own positions and fight with the advantages in our favor.*[109]

On the morning of February 21, General Sooy Smith sent the 2nd Iowa Cavalry, the 6th Illinois Cavalry and a detachment of artillery from Battery K, 1st Illinois Light Artillery, west of town to make a demonstration against the Confederates at Ellis Bridge. The purpose of this Federal brigade was to keep the Confederates occupied while the rest of Sooy Smith's command began an orderly retrograde movement toward Okolona. In order to do this, they had to keep the Confederates, who were defending Ellis Bridge, pinned down at the bridge so they would not harass their retreat.

After a night of preparation for an attack, Jeffrey Forrest's brigade was awaiting the approach of the enemy. Private William D. Howell, Company I, 3rd Mississippi Cavalry, described in his pocket diary his night at Ellis Bridge before the fight: "We laid in line of battle all last night in front of Sakatonchee Creek at Ellis Bridge."[110]

SHOTS FIRED

When the Federals closed in on the bridge, they dismounted from their horses and sent them to the rear. Cavalry learned to protect their mounts by fighting on foot; Forrest also utilized this practice with his men. The Federals then advanced down the road toward the bridge. Attacking Colonel Forrest's troops at about 8:00 a.m., they skirmished with the Confederates for nearly two hours before breaking off the fight at about 10:00 a.m. According to General Forrest's reports, the Federals lost a considerable number of men.[111]

Lieutenant Colonel W.P. Hepburn, commanding the 2nd Iowa Cavalry, reported on the morning of February 21 that one battalion of the 6th Illinois Cavalry, under the command of Major Whitsit, was ordered to reconnoiter the West Point–Houston Road. They ran into a superior force of Confederates about three or four hundred yards from the bridge. The 6th Illinois reinforced the 2nd Iowa. According to Lieutenant Colonel Hepburn, "the enemy was driven across the Sakatonchee."[112]

Datus Coon, major of the 2nd Iowa, reported that he was ordered to take the 2nd Iowa and make a demonstration at the bridge:

> *After dismounting four rifle companies, I advanced them as skirmishers under cover of a fence and in close proximity with the enemy's sharpshooters; I then brought forward two of my 12-pounder howitzers and drove them easily from their fences and houses near the bridge.*
>
> *After some two hours' time used in skirmishing with the rifles, and now and then a shell with howitzers, I withdrew, incompliance with orders, thoroughly convinced of two facts, viz, first, that the enemy had no artillery at that place, and second, that the Federal force was at least 4 to the enemy's 1.*[113]

Private William D. Howell, 3rd Mississippi Cavalry, Company I, described in letters to his mother the particulars of the fighting around Ellis Bridge on February 21, 1864. He identified the location of the bridge four miles west-southwest of West Point. According to Howell, the bridge was a good bridge. There was a home located on the east side of the bluff, with the front of the house facing the road. There was a field between the house and the road. The family living in the house fled before the fighting started.

The 3rd Mississippi, said Howell, was assigned the task of burning the bridge if the Confederates had to retreat across the bridge to the west. The night before the battle, the 3rd camped, along with the rest of the troops, two miles west of the bridge. On the morning of February 21, they were ordered to their horses at 3:00 a.m. By 4:00 a.m., they were riding to the bridge, where the horses were sent to the rear. While crossing the bridge at about 8:00 a.m., the 3rd came under fire from the enemy.[114]

Confederate General Chalmers described how on the morning of February 21, an intense round of gunfire commenced on the pickets, who were driven into the main line of battle. While Chalmers was observing the action from his position on the narrow causeway on the west bank of the Sakatonchee, close to the bridge, he noticed Forrest riding up with his escort. Chalmers stated in a speech he gave years later that this was the first time he had been in an engagement with Nathan Bedford Forrest. He was not really sure how Forrest would act in battle. Chalmers observed Forrest as being "nervous, impatient and impervious."[115]

Riding up to Chalmers, who was sitting on his horse observing the fighting, Forrest asked Chalmers "what the enemy was doing."[116] Responding to Forrest, he relayed a report he had just received from Colonel Duff in command of the pickets. The whole time Chalmers and Forrest were discussing the situation, bullets were "falling pretty thick in the road."[117] The Federals were in a position where they could "readily fire at anyone crossing on the bridge."[118] Chalmers felt that Forrest was needlessly exposing himself to enemy fire without purpose. However, despite the imminent danger to Forrest and Chalmers, Forrest and "his orderly dashed across the bridge."[119] The bridge was about thirty yards long and was being raked by the enemy's fire."[120] Chalmers had no choice but to follow his commander across the bridge to the east side. Later, Chalmers made the comment that he thought Forrest's actions were "somewhat braggadocio [in his] exposure of himself"[121] but followed Forrest to see what he would do.

BREAKING IN A RECRUIT

Crossing Ellis Bridge under enemy fire, Forrest and Chalmers reached the east side of the bridge unscathed. Once across, bullets were still whizzing by. Some of the Confederates were falling back to the rear. One young private came running by after having shucked all his accoutrements. He had even dropped his rifle and his hat. Forrest saw this soldier running to the rear helter-skelter, so he dismounted his horse, seized the young soldier by the scruff of his neck, threw him to the ground, broke off a branch from a tree close by and "administered a severe thrashing with a brush of wood."[122] Chalmers said later that Forrest gave the soldier "one of the worst thrashings I have ever seen a human being get. The terror and surprise of the frightened confederate at this unexpected turn in affairs, at a point where he thought he had reached safety, were as great as to me they were laughable. He offered no resistance, and was wise in this discretion, for the General was one of the most powerful men I ever saw, and could easily have whipped him in a free-for-all encounter."[123]

General Forrest finally turned the young soldier loose. He pointed him in the direction of the battle, telling him, "Now, God damn you, go back to the front and fight: you might as well be killed there as here, for if you ever run away again you will not get off so easy."[124] Needless to say, the soldier obeyed Forrest's orders.

From Chalmers's remarks in 1879 to the Southern Historical Society in Richmond, Virginia, he said that he saw this incident between Forrest and the soldier illustrated in *Harper's Weekly*. According to Chalmers, this illustration was entitled "Forrest Breaking in a Conscript." After checking with *Harper's Weekly* and the Library of Congress, this illustration does not seem to exist in either archive. If it does exist somewhere, it may have been in another publication. I do know that every book I've read on this battle references this event as having been illustrated in *Harper's Weekly*.

Whipping this trooper as he did was not Forrest's usual way of encouraging his men. Usually, he would urge them on by vociferously commanding them, "Come on boys!" Sometimes he was reported to have said to his troops, "The safest place is over yonder!" while he pointed toward the enemy lines. Forrest's domineering stature was enough to encourage his men forward.[125] One of his men wrote years later about Forrest's demeanor in battle that "his immediate presence seemed to inspire everyone with his terrible energy, more like that of a piece of powerful steam machinery than of a human being."[126]

The fighting at Ellis Bridge crescendoed and decrescendoed like a grand symphony throughout the morning. Once a lull occurred in the fighting, Forrest rode out around the right flank of the enemy with his escort company. The lull convinced General Forrest that the enemy troops were only staging a feint to cover their retreat. He was forced to make a decision based on what he had discovered.

Up until then, there had been periods of heated gunfire that came from both sides. In his letters, Howell wrote that once across the bridge, they took their positions behind breastworks. The 3rd Mississippi assumed the extreme left flank, possibly near the creek, the 5th Mississippi protected the center and the 19th Tennessee protected the extreme right flank. The fighting raged for nearly two hours. During this time, the Yankees, according to Howell, used their two pieces of artillery. They fired eight shots at the Confederates. Howell described the shots that found targets. Three shells went through the bridge, one through the roof of the house and a solid shot through the kitchen. Some artillery shells were flying over the heads of the Confederates into the woods on the west side of the creek. These shells were found years later by loggers harvesting the trees for lumber. They said the shells were embedded in the trees along with all types of rifle shot. Many of their saw blades were dulled or broken while attempting to cut down these trees.

During the lull, Forrest called up his escort company and McCulloch's brigade held in reserve on the west side of Sakatonchee Creek. He left

McCulloch in support of Jeffrey Forrest at the bridge. General Forrest then took his escort company of seventy men and "dashed off through the woods to the flank and rear of the enemy."[127] Swinging out to the right flank of his troops and the left flank of the Federals, across the fields to the edge of and south of town, Forrest was able to get a good look at the Federals to determine what they were doing. The Federals broke off the fight at about 10:00 a.m., retreating back to West Point, where they turned up North Division Street alongside the Mobile and Ohio Railroad. The Federals spent time in town pillaging the stores and homes. Even the Mobile and Ohio Depot was burned, along with warehouses containing government supplies. They then joined the rest of General Smith's forces heading north toward Okolona. The Confederates wounded from the fighting were cared for at Elmwood, a plantation home at the end of South Division, as well as in churches in West Point.[128]

While reconnoitering West Point, the movements by the Federal army caused Forrest to have to change his whole battle plan since the brigade his forces faced at the bridge was only a diversionary force keeping his men busy while the main force retreated north.

CONFEDERATE PURSUIT

Originally, Forrest's plan was to hold off engaging the Federals until he had been reinforced by General S.D. Lee and his forces being brought up from the south. Discovering the retreat of the Federal forces prompted Forrest to assume an offensive position. Carl von Clausewitz once explained that in a battle between two forces where one is a defender and the other is the aggressor, "a defender must always seek to change over to the attack as soon as he has gained the benefit of the defense."[129] Von Clausewitz also said that "the offensive part of the battle should never be completely omitted, and we are convinced that all the effects of a decisive victory may and must be produced by this offensive part, just as well as in a purely tactical offensive battle."[130] Forrest took the opportunity to assume the offensive by pursuing the Federal forces with his escort company. He followed the Union rear with his escort and "a portion of Faulkner's regiment, mounted; also with a section of Morton's battery, supported by a regiment from McCulloch's brigade on foot."[131]

General Forrest had never received any formal training such as that one would receive at the West Point Military Academy or Virginia Military

Institute. All of his abilities were the result of what is known in the South as "horse sense," or gut reaction. Growing up on the Mississippi and Tennessee frontier, Nathan Bedford Forrest learned how to survive. Now he had to call on his intuition to figure out how to defeat Sooy Smith. He knew now that he was going to have to switch from a defensive to an offensive posture in order to put the heat on the Federals. Von Clausewitz, in his book *On War*, wrote that "the army actions on the defensive is generally the weaker of the two, not only in the amount of his forces, but also in every other respect; he either is, or thinks he is, not in a condition to follow up his victory with great results, and contents himself with merely fending off the danger and saving the honour of his arms."[132] Even though Forrest lacked formal training, he still knew what the reaction of Smith would be when he pursued him from the rear. The Federal commander's intentions were to never engage Forrest in an all-out battle. He wanted to get back to Collierville with his army intact. So, Forrest's tactic was to pursue Smith north.

An interesting story was told by Andrew Lytle in *Bedford Forrest and His Critter Company* about the troops Forrest ordered up to follow the Federal army. Forrest's escort company heard its commander's order. In derision, they "growled out in disgust and contempt—'Jesus Christ, those are the Kentucky Go-rillers. They won't fight.'"[133] Colonel McCulloch responded by calling back to them, "Go with them one time and see."[134] These Kentuckians were part of the 12th Kentucky under Colonel Faulkner. Captain H.A. Tyler was to take his company and one company of Faulkner's Kentuckians, which numbered 150 men.

Tyler pursued Smith north, through West Point, capturing a few of the enemy. When he discovered that Smith was retreating, he sent word to Forrest. In the meantime, Tyler pushed north, where he set up a line at the end of two open fields lining both sides of a lane. These fields were in the rear of heavy woods. Both of Tyler's companies were halted and placed in positions where they were protected by these heavy woods.[135] They were about two miles north of West Point.

Both sides had scouts out attempting to determine the enemy's movements. Union troops were retreating up North Division Street in West Point. Along a fence row near North Division Street in the area where a TVA substation is now located, one of the oddest events of war occurred.

John Young of the Confederate 8th Mississippi Cavalry Regiment, who was from the West Point area, had been sent to scout the Union troop movements. Near North Division Street, he hid behind a fence in order to survey the landscape. Young slowly rose up to look over the fence.

The fence line where two soldiers, one Federal and one Confederate, faced off, later becoming friends after the war. *From an article by Rufus Ward,* Commercial Dispatch, *Columbus, Mississippi.*

Unbeknownst to him, a Union soldier from the 2nd Iowa Cavalry Regiment, William Rooker, was concealed on the other side of the fence. Both men rose up at the same time to take a look around. Young and Rooker found themselves looking "eyeball to eyeball" at each other. Not knowing what to do and totally startled as well, they simply shook hands and introduced themselves. They then began talking. Rooker stated, "If God lets me live through this war, when it is over I am coming back. It's the prettiest place I have seen." They then decided that as they had "no personal antagonism," they would each withdraw peacefully.

Rooker survived the war and moved to West Point. He bought a farm just north of town near where he had encountered a Confederate soldier along a fence. Shortly after arriving in town, he attended Sunday services at the First Christian Church. He found John Young, the former Confederate soldier. They became close friends after having shared a unique wartime experience. Besides their friendship, Rooker's daughter, Amy, ended up marrying Young's son, James, who later became mayor of West Point.[136]

Forrest, while in pursuit of the enemy, suspected that they were attempting to find another crossing of the Sakatonchee north of Ellis Bridge. He followed the enemy north through West Point, along with Tyler's detachment of Faulkner's Kentuckians, by remaining on Smith's heels. Chalmers had been ordered by Forrest to remain at Ellis Bridge to keep a line of couriers running to keep Chalmers informed of Forrest's actions, as well as those of the enemy.

At about 2:30 p.m. on February 21, Forrest sent a dispatch to Chalmers noting that the enemy was halted in a swamp in front of him about one mile south of John Walker's place. Colonel Barteau had been ordered to cross the Tombigbee River to move parallel to the enemy. Chalmers was ordered by Forrest to move Richardson and General Gholson up the creek (Sakatonchee) toward Houston. Forrest was deeply concerned that Smith might try to get in his rear by crossing Sakatonchee Creek north of Ellis Bridge, so he ordered Gholson's cavalry in the direction of the creek to prevent the enemy from crossing and get in the rear of the Confederate forces.

While Tyler was making sure that his men were protected from a possible attack by the enemy, he and his men heard a bugle calling forth, "Charge." The sound came from the rear. Tyler's men glanced back to see General Forrest, along with his escort company, coming at a gallop, with Forrest in the lead, which was where Forrest was usually found. Tyler formed his men in column and got in line himself. When Forrest arrived, Tyler said to him, "It is death, General, to attempt to go through that lane." Forrest snapped back to Tyler, "Fall in behind and follow me."[137] Tyler refused to fall in Forrest's rear. He told Forrest, "We will ride with you, but we will not ride far behind."[138]

Forrest, his escort and Tyler's men charged the Federals until they fell back. Following the charge, Forrest commented to Tyler that he had a good group of men. Since he had done so well with them, Forrest gave Tyler his escort company commanded by Lieutenant Thomas Tate. Tyler was ordered by Forrest to stay in pursuit of the enemy by harassing their rear. Forrest left this group at a gallop for a meeting with General Chalmers. Forrest wanted to get Chalmers to move his division up to assist with the pursuit of the enemy.

Remembering the derogatory remarks Forrest's escort made about Tyler and McCulloch's men, Tyler was given the chance to pay them back by sharing the following retort: "Boys, let's see whether this escort is composed of crowing cocks, or fighting cocks."[139] Before they could attack the enemy, Forrest had gone to the rear once again to check on reinforcements being brought up by Chalmers.

Tyler led his command in pursuit of Smith. They drove Smith from the Watkins place to the cotton gin on the Evans place, where a full regiment had made a stand. To counter this regiment, Tyler drove it out of its position by flanking it. Both the Federals and the Confederates made a mad race for Randle Lane half a mile away. The Confederates ran into heavy gunfire from the Federals. They were delivering volleys at them less than fifty feet from the lane where they had made a stand behind a snake fence. The sudden volley from the Federals brought Tyler to an abrupt halt.

Major Datus Coon, after the war, filed this report concerning the fight. At the time, Major Coon was commanding the 2nd Iowa Cavalry at the rear of Smith's column:

> *After having passed through West Point "he says" the firing began in the rear, and increased for an hour, when I was called upon by Captain Graves, who was in command of the rear-guard, for assistance, as the enemy's forces were pressing him and threatened his flanks. One battalion of rifles was dismounted and placed behind the fence and brought into line. The enemy thinking the road clear came up with great boldness. At this time two or three shells and three or four rounds of the rifles checked their movement, and my men retired in good order. From the demonstration of the enemy, I deemed it necessary to dismount another battalion of rifles.*[140]

Not able to stand the sudden volleys by the Federals, Tyler gave his men an order to retreat. Suddenly, he heard a voice amid the gunfire giving the command, "Close in with your revolvers, Tyler, I am here."[141]

Looking around, Tyler saw his commander, General Forrest, charging down the road with his saber drawn. Forrest was thirty feet ahead of McCulloch's brigade. Dismounting his men, McCulloch followed Forrest. The fighting was terrific. Forrest killed a man during the fight. The Confederates drove the Federals north ahead of them. Before leaving his position, Forrest sent a dispatch to Chalmers:

> *I find that the enemy has taken the Houston Road to Winston's farm. I think they are badly scared. I wish you to move everything south of Line Creek and picket the fords. I will follow on until I can ascertain the route they have taken. If they should cross the creek and attempt to move west of Starkville, General Lee and yourself will be in position to follow or cut them off. If they fall back toward Pontotoc I will follow as long as I think I can do any good. Send the 2,000 and move as rapidly as possible with the Light artillery. I ordered Colonel Neely with his force this morning to Tibbee Station. Recall him at once and Bell's brigade provided you find the enemy moving west. Direct General Ruggles to keep scouts out indirection of Decatur, Alabama.*[142]

Not convinced that the Federals were retreating north, Forrest still believed that the enemy troops were searching for a crossing along Sakatonchee Creek north of West Point. He was afraid that they would find that crossing, turn west to ford the creek and get behind him. If the Federals had been successful, Forrest would have had to reverse directions and attack their rear. Chalmers and Lee would have had to slow down Smith by assuming a defensive posture to keep Smith from getting in their rear. As it turned out, this did not happen. Smith continued pushing north. He wanted to get back to Tennessee unharmed.

Sooy Smith still had to contend with Forrest. George Waring, commander of the 1st Brigade, wrote in *Whip and Spur*, "No sooner had we turned tail than Forrest saw his time had come, and he pressed us sorely all day and until nightfall, and tried hard to gain our flanks."[143] Smith was not thrilled about his command turning and giving fight to Forrest. All Smith wanted to do was "push forward and give our rear a free road for retreat."[144]

Forrest's cavalry constantly nipped at the heels of Smith's cavalry. The 2nd Iowa and the 6th Illinois consistently had to fight a rearguard action with Forrest's men. In a sense, Forrest forced their retreat north by keeping steady pressure on them. Not only did Forrest incessantly threaten Smith's rear, but he also put pressure on his right flank with Captain Tyler. Smith had to either turn and fight or keep up his retreat north without giving the Confederates a fight. Smith chose to do both. He had his rearguard choose a good defensive position, stand and fight. Throughout its retreat north, Smith's rearguard would turn and fight in order to buy time for the rest of the army to escape to Okolona. "Smith was learning, as Streight had learned before him, that it could be even more dangerous to run from the Tennessean than it was to stand and fight him."[145] There were several heated skirmishes fought between the two forces from West Point to the edge of Okolona during the day on February 21.

Four miles north of West Point, the Federals picked a position in some post oak timber at the edge of the prairie. The Federal rearguard dismounted and deployed in a skirmish line—a line of troopers spread out taking intervals at least three feet apart in a defensive position. The Confederates drove them from this position to the rear some five miles. The Federals lost 15 killed and wounded. Five miles from their previous position, they halted and formed in battle line again across the mouth of a lane where there was a narrow, slippery bridge and causeway. Nearly 150 Confederates were thrown across the causeway to attempt to drive the Federals out. In this engagement, the Federals charged with a lot of energy.

The spot four miles north of town where both sides fought. *Photo by John W. McBryde.*

Forrest saw what was taking place, so he countercharged the Federals, causing them to give way by retreating a short distance north. The fighting was sharp. General Forrest, who was in the midst of it, killed a Federal trooper with his pistol. The Federal was about to shoot Forrest first.

Forrest confronted fewer than four thousand Federals. He dismounted fewer than one thousand troops, sending them forward as riflemen. They attacked the Federals, creating a heated engagement. As a result of the fighting, the Federals fell back through a stand of woods about one mile, where they entered the prairie. Exposing themselves by entering open land, they took a stand behind a strong picket fence that was half a mile long.

Once four miles north of West Point in a wooded area, Major Datus Coon of the 2nd Iowa made a stand. In his report, he explained how he had Captain C.C. Horton immediately dismount one battalion of rifles and place the men behind a fence. He had saber companies brought up to protect the flank.

Forrest, as he approached this fortified position, broke off a regiment from the main body and sent them to flank the Federals on the right. "He moved upon it with his men in two lines, as soon as the regiment in question became well engaged the Federals giving way, Forrest's men rushed up to the fence and from behind it delivered a galling fire upon their rear."[146] Casualties for the Confederates in this skirmish were eighty killed and wounded. The approximate losses of the Federals to this point in the fighting were two hundred, with seventy-five prisoners taken.

The weather and muddy roads caused extreme difficulty for Forrest's men to maneuver. Besides the road being muddy, they had deep ruts caused by the horses, cannons and wagon wheels. Negotiating the roads was a challenge, slowing down the Confederate pursuit. Unfortunately for the Federals, they were also slowed down not only by the roads but also by the plunder stolen from the citizens of the area, as well as all the slaves who left the plantations. The heavy burdens placed on the Federals made it easy for Forrest to continually attack them once they skedaddled north.

Captain Tyler, north of West Point, faced a rearguard detachment of Smith's troops (2nd Iowa and 6th Illinois) as he moved north. He described what he saw as he approached the Federals:

> *Slight skirmishing continued along the road, but no decided opposition was encountered til a point about six miles north of West Point had been reached. Here I became convinced that we had come up with a considerable body of the main column. There were in sight, as near as I could estimate, about fifteen hundred mounted troops and several pieces of artillery, in well-selected position. The country was open in their immediate front. While just behind them was some heavy timber, which offered good protection, and also prevented me from determining the exact number of their troops.*[147]

Differences in mileage given between different commanders for the same strategic place can only be assumed to be estimates since they had no way then to specifically measure other than by the distance a horse could travel in one day. Usually, cavalrymen could travel twenty-five to thirty miles on an average day. If they really pushed it, they could travel a lot farther.

When the Confederates walked their horses up the road, they thought it was clear until Union artillery belched forth two or three shells that landed among them. Several rifle companies commanded by Major Coon of the 2nd Iowa unleashed a volley of rifle fire toward them. A heavy fight ensued. By the time it was over, the Confederates had lost some troops. Due to this sudden demonstration of firepower by the Federals, the Confederates halted their forward movement. Several Confederates were unseated from their horses by the artillery fire and volleys from the Federal rifles.

J.P. Young of the 7th Tennessee Cavalry, CSA, described years later how they dismounted, a common tactic of cavalry. They attacked the Federals with

Railroad at Loohatten Station (Muldon), where the armies fought each other. *Photo by John W. McBryde.*

an intense voraciousness even though they were outnumbered. Four times their number was facing them. Young said that the 7th Tennessee "forced them back to a position behind a strong, picket fence in the prairie."[148] One of the things that charged the men's emotions into desiring an attack was "the burning by the Federals forces by hundreds of dwelling-houses, and the turning of the helpless inhabitants out unsheltered into the cold, wintery air, and fought with a desperation rarely assumed by them at any other time in the war."[149] "Being assailed in the rear by a regiment; the enemy gave way, and the brigade charging and gaining the fever, opened fire behind it hotly on the rear of the retreating enemy."[150]

The 7th Tennessee, along with the rest of the troops present, remounted and continued its pursuit of the Federals with vigor. The men chased them as much as the prairie mud would allow. During this, the Confederates often collided with the Federals in heated fights.

At one point, both sides collided around the little community of Loohatten, where Highway 25 and Highway 45 cross today. There is an interesting story about the 2nd Iowa as it attempted to repel attacks by the Confederates. A trooper from the 2nd Iowa was killed in a fight there. A member of the 2nd

Land beside the railroad at Loohatten where Confederates and Federals fought. *Photo by John W. McBryde.*

Iowa wrote home to the man's wife to let her know what happened to her husband. No changes were made to the language of this letter:

> *Mr. Joseph Mills dear friend I received your letter of the 12th this morning and you wanted know the peticulars of the deth of Hugh Johnson*[.] *he was killed on the 21st of February on the rode from West Point to Okalona Mississippi and about 8* [?] *miles north of West point and 2 miles from paraia* [Prairie] *station on the Columbus and Mobile Ralerode and within about 30 rods of a man's house by the name of James Renolds north of the house on the rode*[.]
>
> *At the time he was killed our company was on rear guard and had no support and the rebels was on both flanks and charging on the rear*[.] *he was turning round to fire his revolver and was shot from the flank*[.] *he was shot threw the heart*[.] *all he sead is I am wounded an fell from his hors*[.] *when the two men next to him dismounted and keried him a few rods and had to leave him—Isaih Stewart was killed a little further north of Johnson*[.] *we left 25 of our boys killed and wounded that eavning*[.] *where we cold of whipped the rebs without any trouble if General Smith*

A soldier getting cartridges from a wounded soldier. *Library of Congress.*

> *had let us went at them but he kep fallin back and drawed the support away from us so that we couldn't save our flanks*[.][151]

The fighting continued as the Federals kept up their march to Okolona, while the Confederates continued their pursuit. Fighting was incessant until dark, when the Federals arrived in Okolona. Forrest's troops nipped at their heels all the way to the edge of the city. After dark, it was dangerous for the Confederates to keep firing, so Forrest ordered a cease-fire. An incident occurred after dark when Forrest's own men fired on him thinking that he was the enemy. Bullets passed through his coat but did not harm him. One soldier was killed by the same friendly fire.

The Confederates made their camps for the night in places where the Federals had made camp earlier. Campfires were burning, and there was plenty of food left for them to eat. Their horses had plenty of grain for forage. It was like the Federals prepared a meal for their pursuers and then left it for them. Tired Confederate soldiers had to spend the night looking at "the flames of burning mansions, outhouses and forage" south of their position.[152]

With Federals in camp around Okolona and the Confederates camped south of Okolona, the evening was fairly quiet as far as fighting was concerned, although Forrest was ready to get back in the saddle at about four o'clock on the morning of the twenty-second. McCulloch and Jeffrey Forrest's brigade was ordered to continue their pursuit of the Federals toward Okolona. They were ordered to take a road that turned off to the left nine miles south of Okolona. By taking this road, they were to reach the Okolona-Pontotoc road, where they hoped to cut off the enemy's retreat toward Pontotoc. General Forrest and his escort rode toward the front to find out what was happening there.

Colonels Clark Barteau and Tyree Bell were riding northward as close to the Federals as they could without engaging them. Their purpose was to shadow the Yankee movements. Barteau and Bell only had 1,200 men. As the Federals poured into Okolona, Barteau established a position about three quarters of a mile east of the railroad. Eventually, he moved his men forward within six hundred yards of the railroad, and this put his troopers lined up in the prairie looking at Okolona.

Forrest, along with his escort, caught up with the Federals. He constantly hit their rear several miles south of Okolona, keeping the pressure on them until they had been pushed all the way through Okolona. The Union soldiers had drawn up into a strong defensive position on the western side of Okolona. They had formed several lines ready to receive a Confederate charge. A normal stance for cavalrymen was to position themselves in several lines, with one line behind the other. For a charge across an open field, against an enemy, this was the cavalry's normal battle position. The Federals' right flank was on an elevation across the Pontotoc road close to the current Highway 41, and their left flank was resting in the woods.

Seeing that Bell was drawn up in position west of town, Forrest rushed to get to Bell's position. "Every countenance was irradiated with confidence, courage, and enthusiasm, which found immediate expression in loud cheers and prolonged shouts of mingled joy and defiance and Forrest gave immediate orders for the brigade to advance to meet an offensive movement on the part of the Federals, as was his habit and tactics."[153] Seeing that Barteau's brigade was absent and that Colonel Forrest had not arrived yet, and while looking at General Grierson's men lined up for an attack, General Forrest made his decision and issued the command: "Charge!"[154]

Part IV

LOCAL REACTIONS TO FEDERAL OCCUPATION

It was the best of times, it was the worst of times…it was the season of Light, it was the season of Darkness, it was the spring of hope, it was the winter of despair.[155]
–A Tale of Two Cities, *Charles Dickens*

Prior to the Meridian Campaign, General Sherman instructed General William Sooy Smith to "respect dwelling and families as something to sacred to be disturbed by soldiers, but mills, barns, stock stables, and such like things use for the benefit and convenience of your command."[156]

As the Federals continued their trek south, they were not to concern themselves with the homes and families along the way. They were to leave all these alone, concentrating only on those things that could be used by the Confederate army for sustenance, both for the soldier and the horse. What the Federal army could not take for their own use was to be burned.

Unfortunately, when the Northern troops arrived in the Mississippi prairie, they did not obey the orders issued by General Sherman. Soldiers began to systematically loot the plantations by heisting belongings of the citizens. Plantation homes and buildings were burned. Many of the slaves took up the torch, contributing to their share of the destruction of the plantations. Devastation spread across the prairie. Black smoke could be seen rising to the heavens, and along the horizon a red glow could be seen as far away as West Point.

Colonel Waring described an incident in *Whip and Spur* when a Federal squadron was sent to a plantation where a man lived with his only daughter.

Word had reached the Federals that this man had actively aided the rebellion. They were sent to arrest him. When the squadron arrived in front of the home, they demanded the owner come out. Waring said that the man "came, and, sullen, stolid, and determined, but obviously unnerved by the force confronting him."[157]

When the plantation owner came out, his daughter was behind him, dressed in a white dress; her long light hair fell over her shoulders. Seeing the Federals, she reacted with rage. Her wild behavior led her to cry out to her father, "Don't speak to the villains! Shoot! Shoot them down, shoot them down!"[158] The father was driven by the emotion of the moment, and he fired on the Federals. They unloaded their weapons on him, killing him.

The Federals, before leaving the plantation, set it on fire. The girl could be seen wandering around, "desolate and beautiful, to and fro before her burning home."[159] Slaves bundled up their meager belongings and joined the Federal squadron.

A member of the 4th United States Cavalry succumbed to his feelings concerning their behavior in the prairie. He said, "The behavior of some of the troops was rather disgraceful and not as we had been in the habit of seeing cavalry act."[160] Due to Sherman's order to not destroy private property, Smith issued an order that "the first man caught in the act" was to be shot. The same soldier of the 4th U.S. Cavalry constantly questioned the amount of time they spent destroying property. He believed that their time could be better spent focusing on their mission of traveling south to Meridian.

Smith discovered the difficulty of keeping seven thousand men under tow. Many would not conduct themselves with discipline. Like a whirlwind whipping through the troops, they lent themselves to absolute savagery, destroying everything in their sight.

West Point citizens could not help believe they would be next. They started preparing themselves for the arrival of the Federals by hiding everything of value they owned. They even had their servants hide their livestock and the food in their pantries and storehouses. Their intentions were to not allow the Federals to strip them of their valuables, food, livestock and horses.

Meet some of the people who had firsthand experiences with the Federals when they arrived in West Point. They shared their experiences as they lived through the overnight Federal occupation of West Point.

Martha Ann Westbrook Dugan

Martha Ann Westbrook Dugan wrote her account of the Federals in West Point in 1915:

> *Well do I remember the advent of the Federal troops into our little town in the spring of 1864. Raiding parties had gone through the state previously and had passed several miles to the west of us* [Grierson's Raid, 1863]. *These were the first I had come in contact with, and they made a lasting impression on my young mind. At the time I was in the home of my uncle Col. Moses Jordon on East Main Street.*
>
> *In expectation of their coming my uncle had removed out of their way much food stuff, provisions, and yet still left sufficient to make it attractive to the soldiers, which swarmed about our lace the morning of their arrival. The first Federals seen by us were in pursuit of a squad of Confederate cavalry going east and the last firing occurred from the street in front of our house, when the pursuit was discontinued and picket stationed.*
>
> *When search for food and valuables begun a few led by a bewhiskered foreigner, I being commanded to light their way, and wanted to observe their proceedings secured a candle (the usual light when used) and followed their bidding. While those aliens were going through my trunk scattering its almost sacred contents about the floor, I was strongly tempted to apply my lighted candle to his flowing beard but considering the consequences (maybe the house burned) desisted. Small loss of personal property resulted from this search, but the humiliation was almost unbearable. We had hid many of our valuables. It being the day of hoop skirt good use was made of its ample folds and met good success.*
>
> *We slept but little that night though few soldiers were about the house. After these intruders departed a few straggling blue-coats returned in the morning in time to secure the breakfast prepared for us. Their stay was short as about this time the bugle was sounded when the pickets came scurrying in and soon the Yankees were all gone. We saw no more of them. Through it all our faithful servant Adam remained at hand and never out of call and ready to do our bidding and there were many others just as loyal to their "white folks." I found real desolation that afternoon when I visited my home just north of town and where my brother Dick Westbrook now lives. General Smith had occupied the house, his main army camped nearby. Furniture and bedding were scattered over the yard, much carried away. Cattle, hogs, chickens all gone, smokehouse*

> *emptied, fences burned—and this is just a touch of war as it came to many sections of our fair southland. Let us rejoiced and be glad that its scars are almost healed.*[161]

THE STORY OF MRS. C.M. STACY (SCALES)

Mrs C.M. Stacy was teaching school in Memphis, Tennessee, in 1852. She was a widow at that time. She met and married a man named Scales, and they moved to West Point in 1852. In February 1864, news arrived that a raid by Federal cavalry was about to take place:

> *Mrs. Stacy had some of her meat removed from the smokehouse and hid it in her dining room. She writes Mr. Jordan told Charlie to take all the horses and mules and all the Negro fellows to Tibbee Bottom. Mrs. Jordan packed 2 or* [more] *trunks of fine clothes and put them in the wagon too. Capt. Ware and all his fine clothes and jewelry down there. Forrest's brigade had been encamped here for several days but left on the 18th of February. News came on the 19th that the yanks are at Aberdeen and were coming to West Point as fast as they could. Guns could be heard the next morning—and about 4 o'clock the dreaded wretches made their appearance in town. Galloping all over the place going into houses and searching for arms and "Secesh," as they called our men. The yanks helped themselves to 40 of my hams before night. They returned for more that night after having been informed by Adam (a slave) of the hiding place. The negroes were in find __________. The Negroes, women and all, went downtown to join the Yankees but they were not wanted.*
>
> *The fighting was toward Suketancie and around by Mrs. Lem Westbrook's where Grierson and Smith made their headquarters. One or two of our men were killed and several wounded. Several Yanks were killed and buried about here. About, sundown Saturday, the 20th, they set fire to the station house, which was all they burned, but they burst the store doors open, scattered and destroyed what they didn't want and gave the negroes. They first went in and took what they wanted.*
>
> *Sunday morning was a beautiful day and shooting commenced with the light, for our men were all around here. Four Yanks warned me and the children to stay indoors and to lie down on the floor when the shooting started. But the children would open the door and peep! There was a whole*

regiment formed inline of battle back of old Collins and facing my house. You may just imagine, if you can, what my feelings were expecting every moment a battle to be fought over my house. They were shouting all the morning from Mr. Jordan's down in town with long range guns and the Yanks would reply. About one o'clock everything begun to grow quiet and we soon found out they were "skeedadline."[162]

MRS. LIZZIE WILSFORD BURROWS'S STORY

Lizzie Wilsford was a girl of twelve or fourteen at the time of the war. She related in later years her recollections of the Federal invasion of West Point. She told how the Federals were intent on destroying the Mobile and Ohio Railroad:

The news had come to our town more than once the Yankees are coming! Later on came the terrible message "Get ready," which meant bury everything of any value and put your clothes back. This was not a laborious job as our wardrobes were limited to a range of homespun suits which, however, we prized very highly. The Yankees came—They saw, but failed to conquer! They took possession of our town burning the depot and the large house full of government supplies. Our house just above town had a large yard, garden, and field. Almost in the twinkling of an eye, the main army formed a line of battle on every conceivable spot facing east, expecting Forrest to [attack] *them. We were ordered out of our house. They said we would be between two fires. But Mama refused to leave, knowing Forrest had gone west believing our house would be burned, we spent the night looking on at* [everything being] *destroyed Uncle Ad (a negro slave) had buried the meat in boxes in the Westbrook grave which was the only thing we had left to eat. Strange to say, the Federals camped out without finding it. Uncle Ad had carried the horses to Tibbee Bottom. Then he hid the horses and walked home at midnight to see about us. Uncle Ad was afraid we were being burned up. Mama told him to rest and take to his horses and that she would take care of this end of the line. Father regarded him for his faithfulness by given him a home (after the war was over).*

In the following morning we were ordered from home again. Mamma knew by this time Forrest had had time to get his men together and that in probability there would be a fight. Se we obeyed orders. When we came across the railroad crossing on Main Street, we met all the ladies and children at the railroad asking an officer where to go, I think he told them with an oath that he didn't care where they went. About that time all the silverware from Mrs. Baptist's pockets came rattling on railroad track. She had on all of her dresses and the mice had eaten holes in the pockets. Children grew very active and some picked the silver. The Yankees being in line of battle did not dare move, but one laughed and said "so that's where you cooks keep your silver is it?" We proceeded to the log house (to which they had been ordered for protection) and remained there several hours. We could hear the guns at Shuquatonchee Bridge and knew a fight was on. General Forrest had kept scouts firing guns from along the Tombigbee to deceive the Union army so that he would take them unaware.

Forrest's men were in the bottom so the bullets went over them. Two Yankees were killed and for many years their graves could be seen from the road. We were all in the log house listening and waiting the outcome. Finally we saw the advance guard coming in. One of the men was on a crippled house. Mama and Mrs. Turberville (Annie Anderson) ran and pulled the fence down for him with the Yankee picket seeing him though the open hall. (The Union general had placed pickets on every street corner and one in front of this log house belonging to Annie Anderson.) This old house had a cannon ball hole through it for many years. It was destroyed by fire two years ago. About that time the "Skeedaddle" signal was given and he (the picket) disappeared. All the ladies with all the children, swinging to them stood at the corner North Division and Main Street looking at the Yankees in full tilt with Forrest and his men close on their tracks.[163]

MR. FRANK BRAME'S STORY

Mr. Frank Brame, once a citizen of West Point, moved to 3800 Bourland Street in Granville, Texas. He wrote in the *Sons of Confederate Veterans* magazine an interesting story of the Civil War—how the Federals invaded West Point on February 20, 1864:

During the Civil War, I remained at home near West Point, Mississippi with my mother and the slaves on my Father's Plantation. I was the youngest of our family, in fact, was only a child at that time. Father and my elder brothers were in the Confederate army.

...Grierson made his raid down the Mobile and Ohio Railroad, to destroy the large corn depots along that line. General Forrest fell on Grierson's rear

at or near Lon Hatton's [Loohatten] *a small station just north of West Point, on my father's plantation. In the early hours of the morning, before daybreak, I was suddenly awakened from the sound slumber of a healthy child by cursing and screams, and turned the room in which my mother and I were sleeping, full of Federal soldiers. Mattresses had been piled in the hallway and set on fire. My mother was sitting erect in her bed with the counterpane pulled around her, and I was simply frozen with horror, for I firmly believed we would all be killed by the soldiers in our house, as they were smashing the furniture with their carbines.*

A soldier found a small package in a bureau drawer. On opening it, he looked at it for a moment, and then ran over to my mother's bed, and leaning over close to her, he and she spoke in low tones, just a moment, then he suddenly left the room, leaving the other soldiers busily engaged, evidently looking for gold.

A few moments after the soldier left the room, a tall, handsome man walked in, and the soldier suddenly ceased their depredations, and brought their hands up and stood at rigid attention. The tall man immediately ordered the fire in the hall extinguished, and also ordered the premises vacated, and guards placed at the several gates of the year. Then turning to my mother, he gravely bowed and said, "Madam, I apologize for the rudeness of my soldiers, and my pursuer shall assess the damage done your property, and pay you for it. No further damage will be done or offered. Under orders, I am compelled to send what meat you have to headquarters, but shall not move it before sunrise, by which time you may have your slaves take away enough for your reasonable needs. With your permission, I will fodder my command in your wood lot; and use enough of our corn and hay to feed the horses of my command, for all which, I will have you suitably recompensed…"

The circumstances related above were indelibly stamped upon my memory, but years afterwards, on my twenty-first birthday, my mother explained to me that the small package the soldier found in the bureau drawer, and which caused him to come across the room and speak with here, the wife of a Mason, was a Masonic apron of curious workmanship and material that had been in the Brame Family since 1676. He ran quickly to his superior officer, also a Mason, and the result was as I have related above. In the fullness of time I became the owner of the apron, and I now have it in my possession, and although some two hundred and fifty-three years old, it is in a fair state of preservation. It is with pleasing memory to me that the only real part of the war I ever saw, left in my heart pleasing memories of the gallantry and chivalry of the Federal soldier and his handsome officer.[164]

TERRIBLE AIM

A story was told by Mrs. Alice Tipton to me when growing up in the Siloam community. Mr. Louis Shirley was a relative of hers.

Mrs. McLemore's great-grandfather, Louis Shirley, had come from Kentucky and settled on Line Creek in the Osborn community of Oktibbeha County. He owned a large farm and much livestock. On that Sunday morning of February 21, 1864, Grandpa Shirley was highly nervous. He could distinctly hear the booming of the twenty to thirty cannons on the hill overlooking Chuquatonchee Creek at Ellis Bridge. Furthermore, couriers had reported that General Sooy Smith and his army were headed south right toward Osborn on their way to Meridian to meet General Sherman. The Shirley farm was in their way. Grandpa took a big chew of his precious plug of tobacco and went to the barnyard to attend to his ever more precious farm animals. He did his best to herd them to a place of hoped-for safety. Back into the house he strode, exclaiming, "Anything is likely to happen. We've got to be prepared for the worst!" With that, he flung his hat into the fireplace and spat tobacco juice on the bed. His wife and children never let him forget it. And Sooy Smith turned, retreating to Memphis and never crossing Chuquatonchee Creek.[165]

Reading these experiences by citizens of West Point, we can better understand the stresses and challenges they all faced when confronted by Northern troops. While the Confederate troops were stationed all around the area, ready to pounce on the Federals if they made a wrong move, the citizens of the city had to contend with the Federals making camp in and around the town. Unfortunately, these Federals did not mind their own business. Many were interested in plunder. They ransacked houses, looking for valuables that they could take for themselves. The womenfolk were left to fend for themselves since most of the men were off fighting. All they could do to protect their belongings was to hide them in every conceivable and secret place they could find. Much of the livestock was taken south of town to Tibbee bottom, where Confederate soldiers were stationed. They did the best they could riding out the storm, contending with the Yankees until Forrest chased them out of town to the north. As suddenly as the storm had come, it went. All was once again quiet.

CONCLUSION

War is the province of chance. In no other sphere of human activity must such a margin be left for this intruder. It increases the uncertainty of every circumstance and deranges the course of events.

—Carl von Clausewitz

Due to the size and limited scope of the battle at Ellis Bridge, most students of the Civil War would not give the Battle of West Point a second look. Compared to all the other battles of the war, this action three miles west of West Point would not even make a ripple on a pond. So how does this battle fit into the rank of importance for the American Civil War?

The Battle of West Point (or the Battle of Ellis Bridge) is a microcosm of a larger campaign. Even though it played a small part, its contribution to the campaign first became a turning point in Sooy Smith's career. For Smith, the Battle of West Point was like a splinter in his finger. As small as a splinter is, it feels like a log when buried deep in the tissues of the finger. Inflammation around the splinter site develops, causing the splinter to become a major sore. West Point became Smith's sore. He had to choose between continuing his journey south to Meridian or standing and fighting Forrest. However, he did have one more choice he could have made. He could have chosen to turn his army around and retreat back to Tennessee. Smith chose the latter. West Point became the beginning of the end for Smith's part of the Meridian Campaign. For many years, Sherman never forgave Smith for failing to leave Tennessee on time and uniting with him in Meridian. In Sherman's memoirs, he wrote that "General W. Sooy Smith did not fulfill his orders, which were clear and specific."[166]

In response to Sherman's accusations, Smith tried to justify the part he played in the campaign by emphasizing that the enemy had mounted infantry whom they had dismounted and placed in a strong position under good cover and beyond obstacles that could only be passed by defiles. "To attempt to force my way through under such circumstances would have been the height of folly. I could not cross the Tombigbee, as there were no bridges and the stream could not be forded. To have attempted to turn the position by our right would have carried me all the way round to Houston again, and Forrest could again check me at the Houlka swamp."[167]

Smith's account is not exactly correct. Grierson had a force in Aberdeen working on a crossing over the Tombigbee when Smith ordered him to return to the main force. If that force had been given a little more time, the whole army could have crossed the Tombigbee and gone down the east side of the river toward Columbus, destroying everything of value. Smith's change of mind actually saved Columbus from destruction.

While spending the night in West Point, Smith became sick. He felt so bad that he even turned his command over to Grierson, his second in command. After handing over control of his army to Grierson, Smith inquired of Grierson about his plans. Being a go-getter, Grierson informed Smith that he planned to take a brigade and push forward to Meridian. This was not what Smith wanted to hear. He immediately took back his command, issuing orders to begin a retreat back to Tennessee.

Evidently, for some reason, Smith did not have the stomach to fight Forrest. I find it hard to understand why he did not want to push his advantage as far as troop strength was concerned since he outnumbered Forrest at least two to one. He was either scared of Forrest or had no desire for bloodshed. Actually, in this situation, Grierson would have been a better choice to lead an expedition south since he had already led an expedition in this part of the country in 1863. He was a lot better acquainted with the territory, making him a better commander in this situation.

Afraid that he could not complete the mission, Smith either lacked confidence of his abilities, was tired of the expedition all together or was afraid of a head-on battle with Forrest. Smith chose to turn around. Whatever the reason, he lost his nerve and headed back to Tennessee. By terminating his part of the mission, Smith chose to retreat north instead of putting his three brigades in jeopardy of being attacked by Forrest and annihilated.

Maybe the reason Smith chose to return to Tennessee was due to Forrest in his front. Why would Forrest pose a threat to Smith since he had a more superior army than Forrest's? Before this campaign even began, Sherman warned Smith about Forrest: "[I]n his route he was sure to encounter Forrest, who always attacked with a vehemence for which he must be prepared, and that, after he had repelled the first attack, he must in turn assume the most determined offensive, overwhelm him and utterly destroy his whole force."[168] When Smith reached West Point, he was facing Forrest from three sides—right and left flanks and in the front.

Forrest had about 3,500 men in the area. Only about 2,500 were fully armed. He was trying to get arms brought up by rail to Artesia. Facing Smith, Forrest had 2,500 armed men against 7,000 well-armed men. Since the odds were in Smith's favor, Forrest had to resort to other ways to obtain an advantage over Smith.

The first tactic used by Forrest was setting a trap for Smith. He deployed his men in three different places in the area, spots where they all could close in around Smith. Tyree Bell was at Waverley on the Tombigbee, Richardson was at Tibbee Station and Chalmers was at Sakatonchee. Forrest's brother, Jeffrey, along with his brigade, was in the prairie, drawing Smith into West Point. Colonel Forrest's objective was to draw Smith down the West Point to Starkville road to the crossing on the Tibbee Creek southwest of West Point. Once the Federals were stacked up trying to cross the creek, the forces from the other three locations would close in around Smith, trapping, capturing or killing the whole force.

Another way Forrest liked to toy with his opponents was by using psychological warfare to get into the mind of his enemy. In the case of Smith, Forrest purposely allowed some of his men to desert him and get captured by the Federals. The deserters reported to Smith that Forrest had about ten thousand troops in the area waiting for him. Not realizing that this was a ruse, Smith allowed their story to work on his mind. Stories told by the Confederate deserters probably played a part in influencing Smith's decision to retreat.

What made Forrest successful in a fight? He would launch headlong into a battle. He did not believe in paying for the same real estate twice. John Milton Hubbard described Forrest's manner as one "who will strike furiously before the enemy has time to consider what is coming, and with every available man in action."[169] Also, Forrest's men demonstrated that soldiers "fighting on foot, can meet, with good chances of victory, a superior number of veteran infantry in the open field."[170]

General Viscount Wolseley once wrote of Forrest that he, "the backwoodsman, the farmer, and the slave dealing knew nothing of 'grand strategy' but he was at once a shrewd, able man of business, and at the same time thoroughly acquainted with the common-sense tactics of the hunter and the western pioneer."[171] Forrest relied on instinct, which won him battles. He had an uncanny ability to read the actions of his enemies and then counter their movements by offensive actions taken by his men. Forrest's military acumen far exceeded that of his enemy counterparts.

Lord Wolseley shared his views of Forrest's military genius by noting that if "his operations be carefully examined by the most pedantic military critic, they will see as if designed by a military professor, so thoroughly are the principles of tactics, when broadly interpreted by a liberal understanding, in accordance with common sense and business principles."[172]

The tenets of Sun Tzu's *The Art of War*, written centuries ago, were ingrained in Forrest by natural instinct, as was a desire to survive. A favorite maxim of Forrest's was "war means fighting, and fighting means killing." War meant all-out killing to Forrest. His objective was to destroy his enemy. He fought to win, and once he had his enemy on the run, he kept them on the run.

There was one particularly important strength Forrest had when pursuing Federal forces. A Northern general expressed it best when he said of Forrest, "We never know where Forrest is, or what he is going to do, but he always knows where we are, and what we propose to do."[173] Forrest had the cunning and the innate ability to read his enemy's movements and figure out what his enemy was thinking. From the movements of the enemy, Forrest could devise a plan to conquer or check his enemy's movements. He knew how to use the forces he had to win a victory regardless of whether the enemy force was larger or smaller than his.

What a contrast between two generals! On the one side was General Smith, who came across as timid and indifferent by the time he reached West Point. You might even say he was a bit indecisive. On the other hand, General Forrest was quite decisive. He knew exactly what he was doing and what he wanted to do. There were no "maybes" in his vocabulary. He decided on a plan and then executed it. Usually, that meant he was going to attack his enemy steady and hard. In Smith's case, Forrest stayed on his heels all the way to Okolona, attacking Smith as often as he could.

The Northern part of the Meridian Campaign was solely dependent on the generals involved. Outcomes of the expedition rested with the combined movements of both armies. Smith was ordered by Sherman to move south to Meridian along the Mobile and Ohio Railroad. Smith was to tear up tracks and destroy Confederate supplies found alongside the railroad. He was warned about Forrest. When Smith did reach West Point, he briefly stalled. The reason he stalled was due to Forrest's presence on both flanks and in his front. He was not sure how many men Forrest had. He was afraid that he would have to fight his way south. Smith made the decision to retreat back north instead of getting into a heated battle with Forrest.

The Meridian Campaign was disrupted due to Forrest's strong stand around West Point and Smith's unwillingness to either continue his journey or take on Forrest. Since Smith did not link up with Sherman, Sherman's plans to march to Demopolis or even Selma were halted due to the fact that Sherman did not have his cavalry to cover his march.

Sooy Smith's seven-thousand-man cavalry caused considerable damage, based on Smith's own reports. After the Federals returned to Tennessee, the railroads were repaired. A considerable time passed before more grain and cotton could be produced in the prairie. Many of the plantation owners in the prairie lost their labor force to the Federal army. Their homes, warehouses and gins had been burned. Many were left with nothing. The Federals' burnt-earth policy executed against the citizenry of the South, which was part of Sherman's total war theory, had left its mark on the land. This campaign was the beginning of others to follow that would destroy the civilian population of the South.

Grant's and Sherman's philosophy called for an all-out war directed against civilians. Meridian and West Point became the test run for a future campaign. Later, Sherman took the war to the civilian population in Georgia after defeating the Confederates in Atlanta. With his huge army, he traversed the state of Georgia, living off the land and destroying everything in his path, including civilian as well as government property. This type of warfare was first practiced in February 1864 in Mississippi as Sherman moved his forces from Vicksburg to Meridian and his cavalry moved from Collierville, Tennessee, to West Point, Mississippi. Sherman and Grant believed that by forcing the civilians of the South to their knees, they would readily surrender.

The South hung on for another year and two months before the end came. In February 1864, Confederates in north Mississippi defeated Federal efforts to disrupt the lives of north Mississippians. Sherman's Southern Campaign was cut short because Forrest defeated Sooy Smith in West Point and Okolona. Forrest and his cavalry participated in other battles from 1864 to the end of the war. William Sooy Smith returned to Memphis after this

Battle of Ellis Bridge monument, three miles west of West Point.
Photo by John W. McBryde.

campaign and resigned his commission in July 1864. He returned to private life, where he was a very talented and successful engineer.

As an honor to Forrest and all the men he commanded, Mrs. Virginia Frazer Boyle wrote the following poem to commemorate their exploits. It is engraved on the monument to Forrest in Forrest Park, Memphis, Tennessee:

> *Those hoof beats die not upon fame's crimson sod,*
> *But will ring through her song and her story;*
> *He fought like a titan and struck like a god,*
> *And his dust is our ashes of glory.*[174]

Appendix A
Nathan Bedford Forrest's Cavalry Command

2nd Tennessee Cavalry
Colonel C.R. Barteau, commanding

4th Tennessee Cavalry
Colonel James H. Starnes, commanding

7th Tennessee Cavalry
Colonel William L. Duckworth, commanding

8th Tennessee Cavalry
Colonel George G. Dibrell, commanding

9th Tennessee Cavalry
Colonel J.R. Biffle, commanding

10th Tennessee Cavalry
Colonel N.N. Cox, commanding

11th Tennessee Cavalry
Colonel James H. Edmonson, commanding

12th Tennessee Cavalry
J.U. Green, commanding

14th Tennessee Cavalry
J.J. Neely, commanding

15th Tennessee Cavalry
Colonel F.M. Stewart, commanding

16th Tennessee Regiment
Colonel A.N. Wilson, commanding

19th (Newsom's) Regiment Tennessee Cavalry
Colonel John F. Newsom, commanding

20th (Russell's) Tennessee Regiment
R.M. Russell, commanding

16th Battalion Tennessee Cavalry
Lieutenant Colonel J.R. Neal, commanding

Nixon's Consolidated Regiment (composed of Nixon's and Carter's 14th and 15th Tennessee Regiments)
Colonel G.H. Nixon, commanding

2nd Missouri Cavalry
Colonel Robert McCulloch, commanding

3rd Mississippi Cavalry
Colonel John McGuirk, commanding

4th Mississippi Cavalry
Colonel C.C. Wilbourne, commanding

5th Mississippi Cavalry
Colonel J.Z. George, commanding

6th Mississippi Cavalry
Colonel Isham Harrison, commanding

8th or Duff's Mississippi Regiment
Colonel W.I. Duff, commanding

38th Mississippi (Mounted) Infantry
Colonel P. Brent, commanding

3rd Kentucky Regiment
Colonel A.P. Thompson, commanding

7th Kentucky Cavalry
Colonel Ed. Crossland, commanding

8th Kentucky Regiment
Colonel H.B. Lyon, commanding

Faulkner's Kentucky Regiment
Colonel W.W. Faulkner, commanding

14th Confederate Cavalry
Colonel F. Dumontiel, commanding

Willis's Texas Battalion
Colonel Leo Willis, commanding

Appendix B

William Sooy Smith's Cavalry Command

Second in Command: Brigadier General Benjamin H. Grierson

1st Brigade
Colonel George E. Waring Jr., commanding

2nd Illinois (five companies)
Captain Franklin Moore, commanding

7th Indiana
Colonel John P.C. Shanks, commanding

4th Missouri
Major Gustav Heinrichs, commanding

2nd New Jersey
Colonel Joseph Karge, commanding
Lieutenant Colonel Joseph C. Hess
Major Amos J. Holahan

2nd Brigade
Lieutenant Colonel William P. Hepburn, commanding

6th Illinois
Lieutenant Colonel Mathew H. Starr, commanding

7th Illinois
Lieutenant Colonel George W. Trafton, commanding

9th Illinois
Lieutenant Colonel Henry B. Burgh, commanding

2nd Iowa
Major Datus E. Coon, commanding

1st Illinois Light Artillery, Battery K
Lieutenant Isaac W. Curtis, commanding

3rd Brigade
Colonel La Fayette McCrillis, commanding

3rd Illinois (five companies)
Captain Andrew B. Kirkbride, commanding

72nd Indiana (mounted infantry)
Major Henry M. Carr, commanding

5th Kentucky
Major Christopher T. Cheek, commanding

2nd Tennessee
Lieutenant Colonel William R. Cook, commanding
Major William F. Prosser

3rd Tennessee
Major John B. Minnis, commanding

4th Tennessee
Lieutenant Colonel Jacob M. Thornburgh, commanding

4th Fourth United States Regulars (unassigned)
Captain Charles S. Bowman, commanding

Appendix C

General Nathan Bedford Forrest's After-Battle Report

On the Battle at Ellis Bridge and His Pursuit of the Federals through the Prairie to the Outskirts of Okolona

Headquarters Forrest's Cavalry Department,
Columbus, Miss. March 8, 1864

Colonel: I have the honor to submit the following report of the movements and operations of my command against the Federal forces under command of General Smith, in the engagements of the 20th, 21st, and 22d ultimo:

Learning on the 14th ultimo, at Oxford, that the enemy was moving in heavy force in the direction of Pontotoc, and believing his destination to be the Prairies, and from thence a junction with Sherman, I withdrew all my forces from the Tallahatchie and Yazoo Rivers and moved rapidly to Starkville, which place I reached on the evening of the 18th ultimo.

On the 19th, the enemy was reported at Okolona, but his movements or intended course was not developed, and fearing he might across the Tombigbee, I ordered Bell's brigade to Columbus and also dispatched General Ruggles to use all his effective force to prevent them from doing so. At the same time ordered Brigadier General Chalmers, commanding division, to send Forrest's brigade to Aberdeen, or in that direction, to meet and ascertain the movements of the enemy; and also with McCulloch's brigade of his division, and Richardson's brigade, under colonel Neely, to move out to West Point, leaving General Richardson at Starkville in command of all the dismounted men of the command to protect my wagon train, and send out scouts in the direction of Houston in order to give timely notice should the enemy divide his forces and move in that direction.

On the morning of the 20th, Colonel Forrest met the enemy in force and fell back toward West Point, skirmishing with them, but avoiding an engagement. In repelling their attacks he lost 2 men killed and several wounded and captured. I moved over to his assistance with General Chalmers and his remaining brigade, taking with me also Richardson's brigade and two batteries of artillery, joining Colonel Forrest within 3 miles of West Point. Finding the enemy in heavy force, and having been informed that General Lee was moving to my assistance, and desiring to delay a general engagement as long as possible, I determined at once to withdraw my forces south of Sakatonchee Creek, which I did, camping a portion of them near Ellis' Bridge and the remainder at Siloam. After crossing the river a courier reported the enemy as having cross the river 8 miles above Ellis' Bridge, destroying mills and taking horses and negroes. With five companies of Faulkner's regiment and my escort I moved rapidly to the point, clearly designated by the smoke of the burning mill, gained the bridge, and succeeded in capturing the squad, which proved to be a lieutenant and 22 privates of the Fourth Regulars, U.S. Cavalry. Fearing the enemy might attempt to cross at the upper bridge during the night, I ordered its destruction, and concentrated my force at Ellis' Bridge, 3 miles from West Point. This bridge I determined, if possible, to defend and preserve, because it was necessary in the event we could drive back the enemy to use it in advancing on them; and had allowed the enemy to cross it and then succeeded in driving them back they would have burned it behind them, rendering pursuit impossible without heading the stream.

During the night all was quiet. On Sunday morning, the 21st, the vedettes and pickets were driven in, and the enemy reported advancing from West Point in full force. I had ordered General Chalmers to dismount his division, throwing Forrest's brigade across the creek in front of the bridge, while McCulloch's brigade took possession of the south bank of the stream to support Colonel Forrest and protect him in the event he was compelled to retire and recross the stream. Dispatches were sent to General Richardson to move up all his force to the bridge across Line Creek, 8 miles of Starkville and 4 miles in my rear; also to Colonel Barteau to move across the Tombigbee, to keep on the flank, and, if possible, to gain the enemy's rear. I ordered Colonel Neely to move his (Richardson's) brigade at once, and to guard all the ferries and fords across Tibbee River from the mouth of Line Creek to Tibbee Station, sending Major-General

Gholson with the State forces under his command to Palo Alto to watch any movement of the enemy from the direction of Houston. In making these necessary dispositions my effective force in front of the enemy was reduced to Chalmers division, my escort, and two batteries. The enemies attacked Colonel Forrest at 8 o'clock, and after a fight of two hours were repulsed with considerable loss. The hastily-improvised breast-works of rails and logs thrown up by Colonel Forrest greatly protected his men, and our casualties during this fight were 7 men wounded.

As the enemy withdrew I followed them with my escort and a portion of Faulkner's regiment, mounted; also with a section of Morton's battery, supported by a regiment from McCulloch's brigade on foot. Our advance at first was necessarily slow and cautious. I soon ascertained, after a few well-directed shots from our artillery, that the enemy had begun a rapid and systematic retreat, and dashed on after them, sending back orders to General Chalmers to send forward to me, as rapidly as possible, 2,000 of his best mounted men and Hoole's battery of mountain howitzers. I soon came on their rear guard, charged it with my escort and Faulkner's command, and drove it before me. They made several stands, but colonel McCulloch, with his brigade, having caught up, we continued to charge and drive them on, killing and wounding 15 or 20 of them and capturing a number of prisoners.

Night came on, and we kept so close to the enemy that my men mistook each other for the enemy and fired a volley at each other, without, however, doing any damage. Fearing a recurrence of such mistakes, and considering the great risk necessarily incurred in following and fighting a superior force after dark, I determined to encamp for the night and resume the chase at daylight next morning.

Early next morning, the column moved forward, taking a different road. With my escort I came upon and charged the enemy 4 miles from Okolona, and drove their rear guard into town, when I found them drawn up in line of battle and apparently awaiting our arrival. Colonel Barteau, with Bell's brigade, had also reached Okolona, and was in line of battle awaiting the arrival of the balance of my forces. Leaving my escort in line as skirmishers, with my staff I made a circuit around the town, took command of Bell's brigade, and advanced upon them.[175]

Appendix D

General William Sooy Smith's After-Battle Report

on the Battle at Ellis Bridge

Memphis, Tenn.,
February 26, 1864

Sir: Major—General Butterfield kindly offers to bear a letter to you, and as the boat is waiting to start I will write you as concisely as possible without referring to my journal for dates.

I moved the infantry brigade temporarily assigned to my command first on Panola and then on Wyatt, and drew Forrest's forces and attention to these points while I threw my whole cavalry force to New Albany, where I crossed the Tallahatchie without opposition.

Forrest then fell back to Grenada, and I moved on by way of Pontotoc to the swamp at the crossing of the Houlka. Here we were met by Gholson's rabble of State troops, to the number of about 600, whom we stampeded and drove pell-mell across the swamp, which we found held in force by the enemy, There was but a corduroy road leading through it, which was impassable by cavalry and could not be turned. So I pressed a saucy attack upon the line of the road as if to force it, and swung my main body over to Okolona and thence threw off a brigade to Aberdeen, threatening Columbus, and moved the other two brigades right down the railroad, destroying it as we went, tearing up the ties, burning them and bending the rails.

From Okolona to West Point we found Government corn in immense quantities all along the road, and this we burned until there was a line of fire from place to place, I had no means of ascertaining definitely what Government corn was and what the property of private citizens, and could only burn that which was cribbed near the railroad. This I did to the extent of from 1,000,000 to 2,000,000 of bushels. We also destroyed 2,000 bales of confederate cotton; private cotton was not disturbed.

All along this portion of our march negroes came flocking to our lines with horses and mules by the hundreds and thousands.

As we approached West Point, we found about a brigade of the enemy drawn up to meet us. This brigade we drove back across the Sakatonchee Swamp, on our right, after a short, sharp fight.

We advanced to West Point and felt of the enemy, who was posted back of the Sakatonchee on our right and the Oktibbeha in our front, in force fully equal to my own that was available for service, encumbered as we were with our pack-mules and the captured stock, which by this time must have numbered full 3,000 horses and mules. The force consisted of mounted infantry, which was dismounted and in strong position under good cover, and beyond obstacles which could only be passed by defiles. To attempt to force my way through under such circumstances would have been the height of folly. I could not cross the Tombigbee, as there were no bridges and the stream could not be forded. To have attempted to turn the position by our right would have carried me all the way round to Houston again, and Forrest could again check me at the Houlka Swamp. I was ten days behind time; could get no communication through to you; did not know but what you were returning, and so determined to make a push at Forrest in front while I retired all my incumbrances and my main body rapidly toward Okolona, just in time to prevent a rebel brigade from getting in my rear, which had been thrown back for that purpose.[176]

Notes

Introduction

1. Jordan and Pryor, *Campaigns of General Nathan Bedford Forrest*, 35.
2. Wyeth, *That Devil Forrest*, 22.
3. Ibid., 221.
4. Ibid.
5. *OR*, vol. 30, part 4, 710.
6. Wyeth, *That Devil Forrest*, 241–42.
7. Ibid., 242–43. There is some conjecture as to whether this incident actually happened as it was recorded in this source.
8. Wyeth, *That Devil Forrest*, 243–44.
9. *OR*, series 1, vol. 32, part 2, 955.
10. Ibid.
11. *OR*, series 1, vol. 31, part 3.
12. *OR*, series 1, vol. 31, part 3, 731.
13. Jordan and Pryor, *Campaigns of General Nathan Bedford Forrest*, 365.

Part I

14. Sherman, *Sherman*, 414.
15. Ibid, 414.
16. Grant, *Grant*, 463.
17. Sherman, *Sherman*, 418.
18. Marszalek, *Sherman*, 250.
19. Ibid.
20. Ibid., 251.

21. Ibid.
22. Grant, *Grant*, 464.
23. Sherman, *Sherman*, 451–52.
24. Ibid., 452.
25. Ibid., 452–53.
26. Wyeth, *That Devil Forrest*, 271.
27. Chalmers, "Forrest and His Campaigns," 7.
28. Ibid., 7.
29. Ibid., 7.
30. Ibid., 8.
31. *OR*, series 1, vol. 31, part 3, 443–46, 449–56, 473.
32. Chalmers, "Forrest and His Campaigns," 8.
33. *OR*, series 1, vol. 32, part 2, 612–13.
34. Ibid.
35. Ibid.
36. *OR*, series 1, vol. 32, part 2, General Orders No. 3.
37. Ibid.
38. Jordan and Pryor, *Campaigns of General Nathan Bedford Forrest*, 382.
39. Ibid.
40. Ibid., 383.
41. Ibid., 384.
42. Chalmers, "Forrest and His Campaigns," 8.
43. *OR*, series 1, vol. 32, part 2, 348.
44. *OR*, series 1, vol. 32, part 1, 348.
45. Jordan and Pryor, *Campaigns of General Nathan Bedford Forrest*, 386.
46. *OR*, series 1, vol. 32, part 1, 348–49.
47. Ibid., 349.
48. Jordan and Pryor, *Campaigns of General Nathan Bedford Forrest*, 386.
49. Lytle, *Bedford Forrest*, 260.
50. Ibid., 260.
51. Ibid.
52. Jordan and Pryor, *Campaigns of General Nathan Bedford Forrest*, 387, from the notes of Captain Walter A. Goodman, AAG.
53. *OR*, series 1, vol. 32, part 1, 282–83.
54. Ibid., 387.

Part II

55. Waring, *Whip and Spur*, 105
56. *OR*, series 1, vol. 32, part 1, 199.
57. Waring, *Whip and Spur*, 109.
58. *OR*, series 1, vol. 32, part 1, 266.
59. Ibid.
60. Ibid.

61. Ibid.
62. Ibid., 267.
63. *OR*, series 1, vol. 32, part 1, 287.
64. Ibid., 288.
65. Ibid., 257.
66. Ibid., 291.
67. Ibid., 299.
68. *OR*, series 1, vol. 32, part 1, 348.
69. Ibid., 349.
70. Ibid.
71. Ibid.
72. *OR*, series 1, vol. 32, part 2, 742.
73. Ibid., 753–54.
74. *OR*, series 1, vol. 32, part 1, 349–50.
75. Ibid., 350.
76. Ibid.
77. Ibid.
78. Ibid., 352.
79. Ibid.
80. Young, *Seventh Tennessee Cavalry*, 75.
81. Ibid.
82. *OR*, series 1, vol. 32, part 2, 784.
83. Mathes, *General Forrest*, 178.
84. Ibid., 179.
85. *OR*, series 1, vol. 32, part 1, 352.
86. *On the Map 145 Years*, 52.
87. *OR*, series 1, vol. 32, part 1, 352.
88. Chalmers, "Forrest and His Campaigns."
89. Jordan and Pryor, *Campaigns of General Nathan Bedford Forrest*, 389.
90. Ibid., 390.
91. Wyeth, *That Devil Forrest*, 277.
92. Clay County History Book Committee, *History of Clay County*, 9.

PART III

93. Hurst, *Nathan Bedford Forrest*, 149.
94. *OR*, series 1, vol. 32, part 2, 267.
95. Ibid., 257.
96. Foster, *Sherman's Mississippi Campaign*, 136.
97. Smith's report in *OR*, series 1, vol. 32, part 1, 252–53, 257.
98. *OR*, series 1, vol. 32, part 1, 293.
99. Chalmers, "Forrest and His Campaigns," 8.
100. Ibid.
101. Ibid.

102. See T.M. Moseley's 1926 map.
103. Wyeth, *That Devil Forrest*, 277–78.
104. Garrison, *Encyclopedia of Civil War Usage*, 255.
105. Ibid., 191.
106. *OR*, series 1, vol. 32, part 1, 352.
107. Ibid.
108. Ibid.
109. Ibid., 257.
110. William D. Howell Collection, University of Mississippi Library Special Collections.
111. Growing up in the area, the author was told by locals that the Federals were buried in shallow graves on the Harter place beside the road until after the war, when they were exhumed and moved to Shiloh.
112. *OR*, series 1, vol. 32, part 1, 291.
113. Ibid., 299–300.
114. Letters in Special Collections at University of Mississippi.
115. Chalmers, "Forrest and His Campaigns," 9.
116. Ibid., 9.
117. Lytle, *Bedford Forrest*, 262.
118. Ibid., 262.
119. Ibid., 262.
120. Chalmers, "Forrest and His Campaigns," 9.
121. Ibid.
122. Ibid.
123. Wyeth, *That Devil Forrest*, 279.
124. Ibid.
125. Foote, *Civil War*, vol. 2, 931–32.
126. Henry, *First with the Most*, 226.
127. Chalmers, "Forrest and His Campaigns," 9.
128. Ibid.
129. Von Clausewitz, *On War*, 400.
130. Ibid.
131. *OR*, series 1, vol. 32, part 1, 353.
132. Von Clausewitz, *On War*, 403.
133. Lytle, *Bedford Forrest*, 263.
134. Ibid.
135. Ibid.
136. Ward, "Ask Rufus: Peaceful Withdrawal."
137. Lytle, *Bedford Forrest*, 264.
138. Ibid.
139. Ibid.
140. Wyeth, *That Devil Forrest*, 281.
141. Lytle, *Bedford Forrest*, 264.
142. *OR*, series 1, vol. 32, part 2, 788 (at the James Evans place, two and a half miles north of West Point, February 21, 1864).

143. Waring, *Whip and Spur*, 117.
144. Ibid.
145. Foote, *Civil War*, vol. 2, 932.
146. Wyeth, *That Devil Forrest*, 391.
147. Ibid., 281.
148. Young, *Seventh Tennessee Cavalry*, 76.
149. Ibid., 76–77.
150. Ibid.
151. Hugh Johnson papers, March 23, 1864.
152. Jordan and Pryor, *Campaigns of General Nathan Bedford Forrest*, 392.
153. Ibid., 393.
154. The rest of this story can be found in a book by Brandon Beck entitled *The Battle of Okolona* (The History Press, 2009).

PART IV

155. Dickens, *Tale of Two Cities*, 1.
156. *OR*, series 1, vol. 32, part 1, 181–82.
157. Waring, *Whip and Spur*, 113–14.
158. Ibid., 114.
159. Ibid.
160. Foster, *Sherman's Mississippi Campaign*, 133.
161. Dugan, "Grierson's Raid at West Point."
162. C.M. Stacy Special Collections, Mitchell Memorial Library.
163. "Wilsford Story," Local History Room, Bryan Public Library.
164. *West Point Times Leader*, February 8, 1929.
165. *On the Map 145 Years*, 53.

CONCLUSION

166. Sherman, *Sherman*, 423.
167. *OR*, series 1, vol. 32, part 1, 252.
168. Sherman, *Sherman*, 418.
169. Henry, *First with the Most*, 213.
170. Ibid., 223.
171. Henry, *As They Saw Forrest*, 32.
172. Ibid.
173. Ibid., 43.
174. Poem by Mrs. Virginia Frazer Boyle on the monument to General Forrest in Forrest Park, Memphis, Tennessee.

APPENDIX C

175. *OR*, series 1, vol. 32, part 1.

APPENDIX D

176. *OR*, series 1, vol. 32, part 1.

Bibliography

Books

Ballard, Michael B. *The Civil War in Mississippi: Major Campaigns and Battles.* Oxford: University Press of Mississippi, 2011.

Bearss, Margie Riddle. *Sherman's Forgotten Campaign: The Meridian Expedition.* Baltimore, MD: Gateway Press Inc, 1987.

Beck, Brandon H. *The Battle of Okolona: Defending the Missisippi Prairie.* Charleston, SC: The History Press, 2009.

Clausewitz, Carl von. *On War.* New York: Barnes and Noble Books, 1832.

Clay County History Book Committee. "Civil War Comes." *History of Clay County, Mississippi.* Dallas, TX: Curtis Media Corporation, 1988.

Cooke, Philip St. George. *Cavalry Tactics or Regulations for the Instruction, Formations and Movements of the Cavalry.* Philadelphia: J.B. Lippincott & Company, 1861.

Dickens, Charles. *A Tale of Two Cities.* New York: Scholatic Book Services, 1962.

Foote, Shelby. *The Civil War, a Narrative: Fredericksburg to Meridian.* New York: Vintage Books, 1986.

Foster, Buck T. *Sherman's Mississippi Campaign.* Tuscaloosa: University of Alabama Press, 2006.

Garrison, Webb, with Cheryl Garrison. *The Encyclopedia of Civil War Usage.* Nashville, TN: Cumberland House, 2001.

Grant, Ulysses S. *Grant: Personal Memoirs of U.S. Grant, Selected Letters 1839–1865.* New York: Library of America, 1990.

Henry, Robert Selph. *As They Saw Forrest.* Jackson, TN: McCowat-Mercer Press Inc., 1956.

———. *First with the Most.* New York: Mallard Press, 1991.

Hubbard, John Milton. *Notes of a Private.* St. Louis, MO: Nixon-Jones Printing Company, 1911.

Hugh Johnson Papers, March 23, 1864. In possession of great-great-grandson, Hugh Johnson, with a copy in possession of the author.

Hurst, Jack. *Nathan Bedford Forrest: A Biography.* New York: Alfred A. Knopf, 1993.

Jordan, Thomas Jordan, General, and J.P. Pryor. *The Campaigns of General Nathan Bedford Forrest and of Forrest's Cavalry.* New York: Da Capo Press, 1996.

Kastler, Shane E. *Nathan Bedford Forrest's Redemption.* Gretna, LA: Pelican Publishing Company, 2010.

Lytle, Andrew Nelson. *Bedford Forrest and His Critter Company.* Nashville, TN: J.S. Sanders & Company, 1931.

Maness, Lonnie E. *An Untutored Genius: The Military Career of General Nathan Bedford Forrest.* Oxford, MS: Guild Bindery Press, 1990.

Marszalek, John F. *Sherman: A Soldier's Passion for Order.* New York: Free Press, 1993.

Mathes, J. Harvey, Captain. *General Forrest.* New York: D. Appleton and Company, 1902.

On the Map 145 Years: The History of West Point, Mississippi, 1846–1991. "Wilsford Story." Dallas, TX: Curtis Media Inc., 1996. Local History Room, Bryan Public Library, West Point, Mississippi.

Rodenbough, Theodore F., ed. *The Photographic History of the Civil War.* Vol. 2, *The Decisive Battles and the Cavalry.* Secaucus, NJ: Blue & Grey Press, 1987.

Sherman, Willliam T. *Sherman: Memoirs of General W.T. Sherman.* New York: Library of America, 1990.

Starr, Stephen Z. *The Union Cavaly in the Civil War.* Vol. 3, *The War in the West, 1861–1865.* Baton Rouge: Louisiana State University Press, 1985.

Tzu, Sun. *The Art of War, Translated with Introduction and Commentary by Ralph D. Sawyer.* Boulder, CO: Westview Press, 1994.

U.S. War Department. *The War of the Rebellion: A Compilation of the Official Records of the Union and Confederate Armies.* 128 vols. Washington, D.C.: Government Printing Office, 1880–1901.

Waring, George. *Whip and Spur.* New York: Doubleday & McClure Company, 1897.

Waring, George E., Jr., Colonel, 4th Missouri Cavalry, USV, Commanding Brigade. "The Sooy Smith Expedition (February 1864)." *Battles and Leaders of the Civil War.* Vol. 4. Edited by Robert Underwood Johnson and Clarence Clough Buel. Secaucus, NJ: Castle, 1883.

Wills, Brian Steel. *A Battle from the Start: The Life of Nathan Bedford Forrest.* New York: Harper Collins, 1992.

———. *The Confederacy's Greatest Cavalryman: Nathan Bedford Forrest.* Lawrence: University Press of Kansas, 1992.

Wyeth, John Allan. *That Devil Forrest.* Baton Rouge: Louisiana State University Press, 1989.

Young, J.P. *The Seventh Tennessee Cavalry, Confederate: A History.* Nashville, TN: Publishing House of the M.E. Church South, 1890.

MAPS

Annand, George. *Map of the Meridian Campaign.* Darien, CT, n.d.

Moseley, T.M. *Map, 1906.* Bryan Public Library, West Point, MS.

U.S. Geological Survey. *Satellite Map 5 km West of West Point, Mississippi.* TerraServer image, West Point, Mississppi, February 17, 1996.

PERIODICALS

Hills, Colonel Parker. "And Then I Rode Right Over Him!" *Guard Detail* (n.d.): 10–16.

New York Daily Tribune. "Important from Mississippi: Return of General Smith's Expedition." March 1, 1864, 1.

Palo, Rani-Villem. "Forrest's Okolona Victory, Feb. 22, 1864." *Civil War Times Illustrated* 24, no. 2 (1985): 32–39.

Philadelphia Inquirer. "General Smith's Cavalry Expedition." March 2, 1864, 1.

———. "Lastest Southern News." March 3, 1864, 1.

Ward, Rufus. "Ask Rufus: Peaceful Withdrawal: 'No Personal Antagonism.'" *Commercial Dispatch,* June 11, 2011, 3..

West Point Times Leader. February 8, 1929.

COLLECTED HOLDINGS

Bryan Public Library. "Captain Cox's Company Goes into Action." Folder 18. West Point, Mississippi, n.d.

C.M. Stacy Special Collections. Mitchell Memorial Library, Mississippi State University.

Clay County Courthouse Land Deeds. "Land Deed Susan and Daniel Ellis," April 1889.

Dugan, Martha Ann Westbrook. "Grierson's Raid at West Point, 1915." Dugan Letters, Bryan Public Library, West Point, Mississippi.

Mathes, J.H. "Battle of West Point." Folder 18. Bryan Public Library, West Point, Mississippi, n.d.

Moseley, T.M. "Writings and Collections." Includes "Wars—Civil War—Clay County," typescript probably by Mosely. Also includes letters to Moseley from Mrs. L.C. Crump, Mrs. Burrows, Mrs. Stacy and Mr. M.A. White. Bryan Public Library, West Point, Mississippi, n.d.

William D. Howell Papers. University of Mississippi Library, Special Collections, Oxford, Mississippi.

Williams, Ruth White. "Battle of West Point." Bryan Public Library, West Point, Mississippi, 1978–79.

Websites

Bearss, Edwin C. "Forrest Gets the Bulge on Sooy Smith." Gatehouse Press, January 16, 2012. www.gatehouse-press.com/?p=389.

The Brockway Family Website. "The Family Journal of the Horton Family of Iowa, Part II." http://www.brockwayfamily.com/Journal/Horton/part2.htm.

Brown, Andrew. "The Hoofbeats of Forrest I." Rootsweb. Ancestry.com. http://www.rootsweb.ancestry.com/~mscivilw/history/hoofbeats.htm.

Chalmers, General J.R. "Forrest and His Campaigns." *Southern Historical Society Papers* 7, no. 10 (October 1879). Accessed at Civil War Home. http://www.civilwarhome.com/forrestcampaigns.htm.

Gianos-Steinberg, Jonathan. "Assessing Civil War Historiography and Nathan Bedford Forrest's Place in It." American Civil War, May 12, 2005. http://americancivilwar.com/authors/NBF.html.

About the Author

Growing up in the city of Memphis and frequently playing in the park that honored Forrest, John McBryde did not know the significance of Nathan Bedford Forrest. When he was eight years old, his family moved to West Point, Mississippi, where they settled. His life was spent in West Point during his formative years. When in junior high, he began hearing stories told by the older members of the community about General Forrest. These stories piqued his interest in reading about Forrest. When he attended West Point High School, he began reading many books about Civil War leaders and major battles. His love for history took a rest while he attended junior college at Wood Junior College in Mathiston, Mississippi, from 1968 to 1970. He graduated from Wood with an Associate of Arts degree. From Wood, he attended Delta State University in Cleveland, Mississippi, where he originally planned to become a teacher but ended up receiving a Bachelor of Arts degree in history.

For seven years, he served as a pastor in the United Methodist Church. While serving as a pastor, he received training as an emergency medical technician (EMT). After serving on a volunteer ambulance service for one year, he decided that his calling was in emergency medicine. In 1984, he went to work for the West Point Fire Department, where he worked as an EMT and firefighter. He also joined the Sons of Confederate Veterans during this time and became a member of first the Chickasaw Guards camp in Houston, Mississippi, and then helped organize a camp in West Point, the Holt Collier SCV Camp, serving as its commander. During the years he served on the fire department, he began researching the Battle of West Point, which turned into a twenty-eight-year project.

After twenty-three years in the fire department, he became the program director and instructor for the paramedic program at East Mississippi Community College. While an instructor at EMCC, he began putting all of his research into a book. Now that research is included in this work. This book is a culmination of many years of research during which he became very familiar with Nathan Bedford Forrest, whom he first met sitting on his horse King Phillip as a statue in Memphis, Tennessee.